HUDSON VALLEY SPCA

Semper Fidelis

ADVANCE PRAISE
FOR *SEMPER COOL*

"Barry Fixler, a Jewish kid from suburban Long Island, N.Y., joined the Marine Corps when he was 18 years old because he believed he needed discipline; he was right. The result is *Semper Cool*, which I recommend be submitted for a Pulitzer Prize. The book is an incredibly detailed account of the making of a United States Marine. Youthful hormones permeate it. Fixler's Vietnam buddies are always tired, hungry or horny. The crotch 'crabs' tale is worth the price of the book."

—TOM "T.J." COLLINS, RETIRED JOURNALIST,
CBS EVENING NEWS AND *NEWSDAY*

"If 'War is Hell,' Barry Fixler discovered an even grimmer inferno in Vietnam. A riveting, incomparable, firsthand account of a combat Marine's experiences and the intriguing aftermath effects on a young warrior."

—SELWYN RAAB, AUTHOR OF NEW YORK TIMES BEST SELLER *FIVE FAMILIES*

"Just finished *Semper Cool* by Barry Fixler. I enjoyed it very much and literally couldn't put it down. It's a very gritty story, a no-holds-barred account of a young man's journey from the comforts of suburban Long Island to the killing machine of Vietnam and back. I can't believe that Mr. Fixler remembers details of what most normal people would repress, and actually has the courage to write honestly about them. This man is wired differently from most people! Painful but riveting! Not a skeleton left in this guy's closet! Loved the book!"

—HATTIE FINKEL, ADVANCE READER

"Incredible read!!! My husband bought the book, but I grabbed it and couldn't put it down. Many thanks to Barry for providing a 'no-whine zone' and several hours of fantastic reading!"

—JOAN O'MALLEY, ADVANCE READER

"I enjoy reading memoirs because it provides me an authentic learning of life's experiences. This was no exception. *Semper Cool* is a great reading. Mr. Fixler's chronicle is both sad and funny at the same time while making me stop and think of the gut-wrenching horrors of war. He transitions easily between vignettes of his personal life and his Marine Corps adventures with a mixture of obscenity and good humor. I laughed at his self-deprecating humor and felt touched by some heart-warming and sometimes emotional incidents he shares with readers."

—JOHN MELICAN, ADVANCE READER

"The vivid description of the Siege at Khe Sanh was outstanding. I finished the book several weeks ago and I still remember reading about Fixler falling out of the helicopter and landing on mailbags that were not picked up because nobody wanted to die trying to retrieve them. I enjoyed his book immensely, and an American such as me should be as proud of the Marines and our country as is Barry Fixler. I salute him. It is a must reading for any American, not only history buffs. I will highly recommend this book to anybody."

—HANK LEVINE, ADVANCE READER

"I was particularly tweaked by the story of when Fixler fell off the helicopter and onto the mailbags, since I was one of the three men who were caught on that chopper and watched him fall. I offer any and all assistance in telling the story, because reading it is the ONLY way people will fully understand what we went through. Give any and all credit to those we served with, particularly the ones who aren't able to get any credit for the sacrifices. Semper Fidelis!!!"

—LARRY MCCARTNEY, ADVANCE READER

"I finished *Semper Cool* in three sessions. The chapters are short, but I blew through 25 on the first night. It is excellent! This book conveys to the reader the horrors of the Vietnam War by as told by a man who lived the story for 13 months and lived to share it. As much as it might be tough for some readers to handle, it's reality, and if this book gives just one or two people a better understanding of what our veterans went through—and it will—then it's a winner. On a lighter note, Fixler gives his readers a few good laughs in describing his antics prior to and after Vietnam. A combat Marine hiding under a bed?!"

—DICK MILLS, ADVANCE READER

"I just finished reading *Semper Cool* by Barry Fixler. I thoroughly enjoyed this firsthand account of this hero Marine and his 13 months of serving in Vietnam. The success and tragedy that he witnessed is clearly described in this extremely well-written book. This is a must read for anyone interested in the Vietnam era. Congratulations to a great Marine and a great and generous American."

—FRED BLOOM, ADVANCE READER

"Semper Cool is addictive. The reader gets hooked immediately and just can't get enough, making this a very fast read. It is also an intriguing psychological glimpse into the mind of a true American hero. Highly recommended for anyone interested in the Vietnam War or who wants an exciting, real-life adventure story. With so much controversy still surrounding Vietnam, and the way veterans are often portrayed in the media, it is refreshing to hear from a veteran who is optimistic, positive and proud of having served his country."

—THOMAS J. NARDI, PH.D. PSYCHOLOGIST AND DIRECTOR, NEW YORK CENTER FOR ECLECTIC COGNITIVE BEHAVIOR THERAPY

SEMPER COOL

ONE MARINE'S FOND
MEMORIES OF VIETNAM

BARRY FIXLER

EXALT PRESS
NEW YORK

Published by Exalt Press New York, LLC. This book is available at special quantity discounts for fundraising, educational or sales promotional use. Visit our Web site: www.exaltpress.com.

All photos courtesy of the author unless otherwise noted.

**Publisher's Cataloging-in-Publication
(Provided by Quality Books, Inc.)**
Fixler, Barry.
    Semper cool : one marine's fond memories of Vietnam /
Barry Fixler. — 1st ed.
    p. cm.
    LCCN 2010933990
    ISBN-13: 978-0-9825184-0-3
    ISBN-10: 0-9825184-0-4

    1. Fixler, Barry. 2. Vietnam War, 1961-1975—
Veterans—Biography. 3. Marines—Biography. 4. Vietnam
War, 1961-1975—Personal narratives.   I. Title.

DS560.72.P39F59 2010   959.704'3'092
                      QBI10-600160

Cover design by John Hamilton
Page design by Ryan Scheife

First Edition
10 9 8 7 6 5 4 3 2 1

For Mitch Sandman
and Mike Lucas

CONTENTS

I.   IN HARM'S WAY 1

II.   MAKING A MARINE 17

III.   INTO THE FIRE 53

IV.   KHE SANH 115

V.   NO SLACK FOR A SHORT-TIMER 165

VI.   COMING HOME 187

VII.   CALLS TO DUTY 223

Author's Note and Acknowledgments 245

POW/MIA Recognition 247

INTRODUCTION

You might wonder why I titled this book *Semper Cool: One Marine's Fond Memories of Vietnam*. How, you might ask, could I have fond memories of Vietnam? I saw Marines severely wounded or killed on a regular basis. I endured the horrible hardships of combat. How could I have fond memories?

There is no doubting that I am a very lucky man. At most reunions with my war buddies, I'm usually the only one without a Purple Heart, which is awarded to those wounded in combat.

Somehow I made it through the Siege of Khe Sanh and the worst that Vietnam could throw at me and suffered little more than a scratch, when men all around me were wounded or killed.

I look at myself today, and I'm in great shape. I came home from Vietnam mentally and physically sound, and that is reason enough to have fond memories.

Since Vietnam, I've had success in life and in business, and to this day, I attribute my accomplishments and the way I conduct myself to the values instilled in me by the United States Marine Corps and lessons I learned in Southeast Asia.

Every Marine is responsible for the legacy of the Corps. I never want to be the one who tarnishes that, and still I want to do more. That's why I am pledging all of my profits—100 percent of my royalties—from this book to wounded combat veterans and their families and the children of warriors that were killed in Iraq and Afghanistan fighting for our country.

———

Vietnam was an adventure. Some days were pure horror, while other days were just plain miserable. I saw a lot of death at a young age. Yet, when it all was over, despite the hardship and horror, I felt as if I had accomplished something important. I still feel that way.

I would do everything again in a heartbeat, no second-guessing. Of course, Marines were hurt and killed. I feel terrible about all of the men who lost their lives or their good health, but if I had to do it over again, I would.

The Marines gave me quiet confidence, and my combat experience left me with healthy self-esteem.

I could attend a dinner with New York Mayor Michael Bloomberg, who's a multibillionaire, and maybe a few dignitaries or doctors or lawyers, and I wouldn't feel inferior. I am as much their equal as they are mine.

I am a combat veteran, *a combat veteran*. I helped fight a war and I put my life on the line when my country asked me to. That's all the confidence I need to hold my own in any group.

I joined the Marine Corps in part to earn my father's respect. I grew up hearing all of his Army stories from World War II in the Pacific and how in awe he was of the Marines. My dad was proud of my service, and that means the world to me, and I am proud of the men and women who continue to risk their lives to defend our country and the ideals it stands for.

IN HARM'S WAY

1

Good Morning to an Automatic

"Don't move or I'll fucking kill you!"

The big guy in the black trench coat across the counter of my jewelry store shoved an automatic pistol into my face and screamed while his partner in white stood to his side.

"I'll fucking kill you! Don't move or I'll fucking kill you!"

I don't like automatic pistols, so I moved.

Valentine's Days are usually great if you're a jeweler. Guys come in from morning to night picking out something for their girls: engagement rings, necklaces, earrings, last-minute gifts from the heart, the things they buy when they're in love. It's one of a jeweler's biggest business days of the year.

I'm Barry Fixler. I'm a jeweler, just like my father Louis before me. February 14, 2005, was a Monday, and my head was still a little numb from a weekend of celebrating when I arrived early at my store, Barry's Estate Jewelry, in Bardonia, New York.

I anticipated a typically busy and profitable Valentine's Day as I sorted through new jewelry to display.

3

It wasn't 9:00 a.m. yet and I still had the glass front door locked, though I expected people to come early. They always do on Valentine's Day morning.

I thought nothing of it when two fellas walked up to the door. One wore a white, hooded sweatshirt, and the other had on a black trench coat, but they looked fine to me. No alarms went off in my head. I actually walked around from the counter and unlocked the door to let them in.

The one in black asked if he could see an engagement ring, and then the other guy piped in.

"I tried to talk him out of it, but my buddy wants to get engaged today," he said.

I've heard that a thousand times, guys wanting to get engaged on Valentine's Day. My back was to them as I walked back around the counter, but I have natural instincts.

I kept a few feet of distance between us so that if one of them lunged at me, if they were bad guys, I would be able to hear the rustling or sense the quick movement. If that happened, I had left enough room that I could bolt away.

The guy asked to see a marquise stone. It's an unusual shape, the marquise.

While I showed it to him, the other guy paced six or seven feet away from me. They had arrived while I was still setting out the jewelry in the displays, and the safe in back of my store was wide open. No big deal.

Helping the two guys, I actually got down on my knees behind the showcase because my leg hurt. I thought nothing of it. My guard was down. At that moment, if I had to make the call, I would have said there was no way that they were going to do something to me. I felt no threat.

I showed them the easiest ring to reach, and I noticed the price tag: $11,500. I saw the guy hesitate. Now I know why he hesitated, but at the time I thought it was because of the price.

I thought to myself, "Jerky Barry! This guy doesn't want to spend eleven, twelve grand. Pick out another stone." I never said to him, "Oh, if you can't afford this, let me show you something else."

That's not classy.

So, without discussing the price, I started looking for another ring in the $3,000 to $5,000 range.

I was really off guard. I had celebrated with family and friends on Saturday night after learning that my mother Ronnie had tested negative for cancer.

That Saturday, it was just friends, maybe thirty or forty other people, and we rented a private room at a restaurant. Each person paid $100, and it was catered just like a wedding: cocktail hour, appetizers, the whole bit.

I took it to another level. I started drinking a martini, drinking a beer. I started dancing. Another martini. Another beer. We all were friends laughing and having a great time.

I had a major hangover the next morning, and on top of that, I had danced the whole night carrying a pistol on my right ankle. The handgun weighed three or four pounds, and I woke Sunday barely able to walk. I don't usually carry my pistol in social situations, but I had been in a hurry to close my store and get to the celebration and somehow forgot I had it on me.

But I'd made plans to go drinking with four or five friends. No women were around, so we all were cursing loudly and toasting each other and having fun when my friend John Settle hit me with a question.

"Barry, what would you do if someone came to hold you up?"

"I'd shoot them. I have no fear," I said. "I have a fear of someone breaking into the store when I'm not there, but if thugs came in armed and loaded, I have no fear of that. I'd just light 'em up."

My friends knew that I was a combat Marine and that they'd get an answer like that, but it was something that they still took with a grain of salt because Vietnam was years ago.

John asked me that question on Sunday. The next day was Valentine's Day, and an automatic pistol was in my face.

"Don't move or I'll fucking kill you!" the guy screamed. "I'll fucking kill you! Don't move or I'll fucking kill you!"

My brain snapped into high gear, time froze, as it always did in combat, and in a fraction of a second I evaluated the situation: "This is the real deal. That's an automatic pistol in my face, and I don't like automatics."

These thugs didn't just pull a gun on Barry Fixler the jeweler. They were threatening the life of Cpl. Barry Fixler, United States Marine Corps, and they weren't the first to do it. If they had known that, they might have rethought their plan.

"Now I have to kill these two guys," I thought. "I HAVE to kill them."

2

Mitch, Crazy Freddy
and Mad Luck

Crazy Freddy was the first person who ever tried to shoot me. That was in the mid-1960s, and Crazy Freddy didn't know he was really trying to shoot me because he didn't know that the pistol that I'd pulled on him and my best friend Mitch Sandman was real.

I was fifteen years old, and that was also the first of many times that I got lucky with bullets. I have such good luck with bullets that I don't actually fear getting in a shootout. I respect handguns and rifles, but so many bullets have whizzed past me that I must be lucky.

My dad carried a revolver, a five-shot Smith & Wesson .38 Special. That model has been around for more than one hundred years. It is somewhat common for jewelers to own and carry pistols.

It was a school night, and my sister Vivian and I were home alone in our comfortable, split-level house that was like so many of the other homes with spacious lawns and neat hedges in our Long Island, New York, subdivision.

Vivian was eleven, so I was babysitting. Our parents had gone out for dinner.

It wasn't a big deal, so I called over my friends Mitch and Crazy Freddy to mess around. My sister was upstairs reading.

My father had left his pistol on his nightstand, so I sneaked around and strapped on the handgun, just as a goof. I wore it in its holster under my robe. When they were least expecting it, I jumped out and pointed it at Mitch and Freddy screaming, "Aaahhh! I'm gonna kill you! I'm gonna shoot you!"

Mitch had been my friend since second grade. He knew the handgun was real and bolted for cover. Crazy Freddy thought it was a fake. He jumped me and tried to grab the gun like he was going to shoot me.

"You wanna shoot me?!" Crazy Freddy screamed. "Now I'm gonna shoot you!"

In a split second, my stupid prank turned into a life-and-death struggle. Crazy Freddy was bigger and stronger than me. He locked his hands over mine, trapping my finger on the trigger while we struggled for control of the handgun. It took all of my strength to keep the muzzle out of my face, and I kept screaming to Freddy that it was my dad's gun—it was real—but he wouldn't listen.

BOOM!

The gun fired and the blast of gunpowder and gas ripped Freddy's pants right off and peppered his legs. The bullet missed him and went through my mother's couch and lodged into the baseboard of the wall.

"Holy crap!" Freddy howled. "I didn't know it was real!"

Then he and Mitch ran out the door, and I heard my sister upstairs crying, so I went up and threatened her.

"Go to sleep and don't say anything to Mom and Dad!"

"Jesus Christ!" I thought, still stunned. "We killed the couch."

Then an idea hit me.

I had a six-month-old puppy, Taffy, and I decided to frame her for the damage. I picked her up and took one of her paws and used

8

its toenails to make the bullet hole in the couch bigger. The trunk of my father's Ford had a bunch of loose bullets in it, so I grabbed one and replaced the spent cartridge.

I placed the pistol back on the nightstand where I had found it and waited for my parents to return. I had the puppy convicted the second that they walked in the door.

"You should see what Taffy did!"

My poor mother wailed. "Oh my couch! My couch! My couch!"

"Yeah, the dog just flipped out and tore up the couch," I said. The puppy didn't know better. I put the blame all on Taffy, and my parents bought it.

It was my first real life-and death situation, and I'm still amazed that Crazy Freddy didn't shoot me in the face, or I didn't blow a hole in his leg. We could have killed my sister with a stray bullet.

But the couch took the bullet and the dog took the blame. It was such a horrible night that Crazy Freddy, Mitch and I never discussed it. We just said, "You know what? That was not cool."

———

Mitch Sandman and I could find trouble without even looking for it. We were in sixth grade when we ruined his mother's kitchen just by making soup. We put it on the stove, started talking and stopped stirring, and pretty soon left the room altogether. We didn't remember until we smelled the smoke, and by then the kitchen was charred and it was too late. There wasn't an actual fire, but the smoke damage was severe.

We always got into jams, and it didn't help that Mitch was made for mischief, and he was an authority on fireworks. He got hold of some cherry bombs in high school and lit one during class while the teacher's back was turned. The thing exploded against the chalkboard and the teacher almost jumped out of his skin. He composed himself, turned around, and went straight to Mitch's desk, because Mitch was always the first suspect when anything like that happened.

His reputation was well earned, and it only elevated him in the eyes of the kids in school. Mitch was A+ cool. He challenged authority every chance that he could, and once even provoked a teacher so much that the teacher lost his composure and they got in a wrestling match in the hall while I stood to the side and laughed.

Cool mattered to me. I always tried to be the coolest kid in class, or one of them. If I wasn't the coolest kid, I wanted to hang out with the coolest. Not doing your homework, maybe cutting up in class, making people laugh, those things were considered cool.

By seventh grade, I decided that my best path to cool was to get in fights.

I was at my hall locker one day between classes and decided that the time was right, so I picked a fight with the kid next to me.

"Barry, you gotta do something cool," I remember thinking. "You have to get in a fight."

I was a shrimp, maybe five feet tall and lucky if I weighed one hundred pounds, and the other kid was quite a bit bigger. There was no grandstanding. I pushed him. He pushed me. Then I threw a punch that missed, and the fight was on.

We swung a few times and he connected with me and tagged me right in the jaw. My head banged against the open locker door. They were the standard metal hall lockers that everyone remembers from school, and my head hit a corner.

I still have the scar. Crack! I went down and my head smacked hard on the marble floor. I was out cold for a few seconds, and the next thing I remembered was looking up at a crowd of kids standing over me saying, "Oooh! Oooh! The blood!"

I tried to get up and get my bearings, but I couldn't stand up, and I was bleeding all over the place. The wound was a gusher. Head injuries do that. I learned that too well later in Vietnam.

A woman teacher rushed over to help me and pushed a gauze pad against the wound. She took me to the school nurse, and they kept trying to stop the blood from flowing. It was all over me.

"Do I need stitches?" I kept asking them.

"Whoa! You need a lot of stitches!"

"Ah, damn!"

Word spread fast through the halls: "Barry got beat up!"

This was a nerdy Long Island public school, not a city school, so it was big news. When I went back the next day, it turned out that I was a hero for getting my ass kicked. I walked in and it was as if I had become famous overnight.

During my senior year, a junior made fun of me in the cafeteria one Friday when he saw me chewing on a napkin. I couldn't let that ride, so I confronted him in the hall even though, like most guys in my school, he was way bigger than me.

"What was so funny?" I asked. "Why were you laughing at me?"

I threw the first punch and landed it, but not enough to knock him down, and then he clocked me and I fell, semi-conscious, and the fight was over. I had a classic black eye by the final school bell.

I had to attend a cousin's wedding the next day, and my mother flipped out when I came home.

"How can I take you with a black eye to a wedding?!"

Because it was a very Jewish wedding, and these very Jewish people didn't get into fights.

I was telling myself, "Damn, this is cool."

I made the rounds at the wedding, my black eye telling all of my uncles and my cousins, "I got balls enough to get in a fight." It was a macho thing. I was loving life, and my mother was mortified.

I never came off as being a tough guy, and my career school fighting record was 0-2 or 2-0, depending on how you looked at it. I was more of a funny guy out to have a good time, but I did have guts—courage—and that counted in the cool department.

Mitch didn't have to try hard to be cool. He was cool by nature. He hatched this plan in eleventh grade to blow up one of the toilets with a block of M-80 firecrackers, and he dragged into the scheme this nerdy new kid who was tagging along with us, hoping that some of Mitch's cool would rub off on him.

I was the lookout, and of course Mitch talked the nerd kid into being the one who lit the fuse while everyone else ran. But he made the mistake of loaning the kid the unmistakable Zippo lighter that he always carried and flicked a certain way to look cool.

The toilet exploded about the same time that a teacher walked in, and the nerd was stuck standing there holding what obviously was Mitch's Zippo. We all got busted, but Mitch had to repeat eleventh grade because of that. It only elevated his coolness in the eyes of the rest of the kids.

But for all of his bravado, Mitch was never a tough guy. He never went looking for fights, and he had no business ending up in Vietnam.

3

Something About the Tracers

The enemy started shooting at me on my second night in Vietnam. My squad was designated as backup for another squad out on patrol. We waited in a semi-secure area; if they got involved in a firefight, it was our job to go out and help them.

It was sometime after midnight, and we weren't very far from the other squad, maybe a quarter-mile or less, but dense jungle and overgrown trails separated us in the pitch dark. We couldn't see, and we didn't want to fall into any booby traps or walk into an ambush.

The other Marine squad stumbled into an enemy trap and called for backup. Air support wasn't possible, and they needed us.

I was the new guy, and everybody knew that I was a new guy, so they didn't expect much from me. Out of about ten guys in my squad, I hovered right in the middle of the pack.

We were single file, spread out about eight feet apart in case somebody stepped on a Bouncing Betty, the land mines that shoot into the air about waist level before they explode. Spread like we were, it wouldn't take out two or three guys, just one.

I was extremely anxious. Scared is not the right word. My

adrenalin was pumping. This was the real deal, and I didn't know what to expect. I found out pretty quick.

The Viet Cong were smart. Only one trail led to where they'd ambushed the other squad, so they figured, "We'll fuck up the backup, too."

We humped toward the area, and my mind raced a million miles an hour. The term "humping" is what we used for hiking or marching on combat patrol. I didn't hear any shooting, and all I could see was the very faint silhouette of a Marine about eight feet in front of me. I concentrated on him instead of my flanks. I was green and I didn't want to get lost. I didn't even care about the Marine behind me. It was my first night patrol, and all I could imagine was my squad leader screaming, "Where the fuck is Fixler?!"

I didn't want to hear any of that.

We walked smack into the Viet Cong ambush. They picked a perfect spot to light us up, a trail as straight as a bowling lane. I heard machine gun fire, and tracers started flying. Every third or fourth bullet on a machine gun is a tracer meant to show where the rounds are going.

Something was strange about these tracers, different than what I'd seen in training back in the States. Everyone else hit the ground, but I just stood there with my M16 staring, not comprehending, not reacting.

Tracers flew right past my head. That was it! They were coming *at* me! It was the first time I had seen rounds being fired at me, and I just didn't react. It was almost as if I was studying the situation, thinking, "The tracers should be going *that* way, *that* way. Why are they coming *this* way?"

I guess I'd thought maybe the tracers were from us shooting at the bad guys. Finally my brain snapped into gear. "Whoa! You're being shot at!"

Then I dove to the ground, as flat as could be, and when I did, I stabbed my M16 barrel-first into the earth like a bayonet. It stood straight up in the mud, and bullets whizzed all around it. I tried to keep my head down and dislodge my M16, but I couldn't get any leverage on it because I was lying as flat as humanly possible.

It was almost a miracle that the stock of the M16 didn't get blown apart. The Viet Cong bullets were coming at us furiously, and my M16 was exposed.

I could imagine standing in front of my squad holding just the muzzle because the plastic stock would've been chewed to bits.

"Fixler's M16 got killed!"

I never would have lived that down.

I didn't feel lucky that night; I felt very inexperienced, bright green.

The barrel of my M16 was jammed with mud for the rest of the patrol, and I knew from training that if I fired it, the rounds could blow up in my face and kill me.

"Oh fuck!" I thought. "I can't even return fire now. There's no way that I can pretend that I am a combat Marine."

You think when you come out of boot camp and combat training that you can rip apart the world. But you find out real quick that you're not about to rip apart anything.

You eventually get used to being shot at, but I wasn't there yet. It was very dramatic to me, but I also was embarrassed.

I would have lowered myself in the eyes of the guys if I had said anything. They'd have just called me a fuck-up.

MAKING A MARINE

4

Planting the Seed

I had life very easy growing up in my mostly Jewish neighborhood in Long Island. The houses were big and the lawns were bigger, and everything was neat and trim.

If I was slow in math, I had a math tutor. If I was slow in English, I had an English tutor. Anything I wanted in life—a set of drums, a guitar, singing lessons, whatever—I got it: my own room, my own TV, my own air conditioner, just everything. I had two cars, a motorcycle and a horse by the time I was sixteen.

My mother Ronnie would scream and holler, but you know, your mom is your mom. I wasn't intimidated by my mother. She could throw something at me and I'd just laugh.

Your father's something different, but my father worked all the time and was not a disciplinarian. With him, punishment was: "No TV for two days, alright son?" Half an hour later, he'd say, "OK, you can watch TV."

My father served in the Army during World War II, but he was in awe of the Marines. He told dozens of stories about them when I was growing up. That planted the seed for me to become a Marine, and the seed grew into a passion.

"What are these Marines?" I would ask myself. "Why do they have such a mystique?"

My father was proud that he served in the Army for the United States of America, and he was proud of us as a family, but he was proudest of me being a Marine, a combat Marine.

If somebody brought up something about the military during a conversation, he would say, "My son's a Marine" ten times before he'd tell people that he served in the Army.

Louis Fixler grew up in the 1920s and '30s as a Jew in Romania and Hungary, very poor, running from town to town. He had eight siblings: four brothers and four sisters. Those were the days of large families. This was before Hitler, but even then in those parts of Europe, Jews were not welcome, and so my father's family fled across the Atlantic when he was fourteen years old. They settled in the Bronx.

By 1940, my father was in his twenties but still had no direction, so he joined the Army on his own, the only one of four brothers who served. He knew he needed to get his bearings in order to navigate his way through the world.

Putting on that uniform was the first time, he said later, that he felt like he belonged to a country. "Thank God I finally belong somewhere! I finally have a country!" He said it was the greatest feeling.

He was stationed in Hawaii on December 7, 1941, when the Japanese bombed Pearl Harbor. He was proud to be a Pearl Harbor survivor.

Louis spent most of 1941 through 1945 hopping from island to island in the Pacific theater, and that was where the Marines that he encountered were etched into his memory.

The Army was much better supplied than the Marines in World War II, my father said. Army guys even received pallets of beer on some of the islands, and that beer was such a valued commodity that the Army stationed volunteers to guard it. But the Marines would get wind of the beer and decide, "To hell with the Army guys."

The Marines would sneak over and take out the sentries—just knock them over their heads or rough them up—and commandeer the beer. They'd just take it. After that happened several times, nobody in the Army would volunteer to guard the beer.

"Are you kidding me?" my father recounted. "We're going to mess with the Marines? Forget about it! Just let them take it! We know we're going to get beat up. Just give the beer to the Marines. They're crazy!"

———

Stories like that stuck, and by the age of fifteen, I had my own story about stealing booze.

A buddy of mine and I had paper routes. We rode bicycles with big baskets on the front and threw newspapers onto the doorsteps and big lawns of the houses in my Long Island neighborhood.

A restaurant along my friend's route caught fire, and after the blaze was out, he rode his bicycle past the blackened building and noticed the charred liquor bottles at the bar inside. They were black, but unbroken, and all of that liquor was just there for the taking.

He pedaled straight to my house a few blocks away.

"Oh my God! All that booze! Let's go! Let's grab it!"

The windows were broken and the place was wide open, with only yellow fire department ribbon to warn people away, but that meant nothing to us. We filled our bicycle baskets with so many liquor bottles that we wobbled on the bikes like drunks as we pedaled back to my house.

"What do we do with all these bottles?"

My mother took great pride in all of the shrubbery around my house, and we thought the bushes would be a great place to hide the booze. We thought that we'd have enough liquor to last us through the rest of high school.

We raided the burnt-out restaurant on a Tuesday and decided it would be cool to wait until the weekend and throw a huge party for all of our friends.

It was late spring, and the next day the neighborhood gardening crew came. A truck would drop off a crew of about ten black day laborers from the Bronx, and they tended to the yards of all of the houses in my subdivision. The truck driver would return in a few hours to gather all of them and move on to another neighborhood.

That morning, while I was at school telling all of my friends about my huge liquor stash and making plans for a blowout weekend party, the gardening crew picked my house to begin the workday. It didn't take the guys long to find one of the hidden liquor bottles, and then another and another. Every man on that crew dropped his tool and converged on my mother's bushes and started drinking. She must have looked out the window and thought that our shrubs were getting special attention.

Mine was a lily-white, mostly Jewish neighborhood, and within a few hours, every man on that all-black gardening crew was rolling drunk and passed out on people's lawns. I can only imagine what went through the neighbors' heads.

The truck driver returned and found his crew shit-faced on untended lawns, and he thought, "What the hell?!" He had to physically lift each man onto the truck. All of the evidence was scattered across my yard, and I got caught.

When the truck returned the next week, the men all swarmed to my bushes, and the boss driver had to get out and inspect them to make sure that no more liquor bottles were there, or he would have returned to the same nightmare.

———

Most of my father's service was in Army communications or transportation units, which were assigned to secure an island after the Marines had taken it from the Japanese. Saipan, Okinawa, Guadalcanal, Iwo Jima… Marines would go in there fighting hand-to-hand with the Japanese like savages, and when things started to settle down, the Army would move in and establish communications bases, landing strips, hospitals and roads.

Only a few Marines would be left on the island by then, and even on the heels of bloody battles, they would still be marching, training, preparing for the next fight.

"How tough these Marines are," my father remembered telling himself. "There's no let up in these guys. Please, give these Marines a break. They're not giving these guys breaks. Army guys have breaks, but Marines don't. What are these guys made of?"

He was in awe, really in awe, and the stories that he told me when I was a teenager impressed me. He told a story about arriving after dark on an island that the Marines had just seized. He couldn't see and didn't know that dead Marines were all around him, piled one atop another… hundreds of them.

"Holy shit!" he said. "What's that smell? What's that rotten smell?"

A Marine grabbed him.

"What the fuck do you mean that rotten smell?" the Marine yelled. "These are dead Marines!"

My father said that he couldn't apologize quickly or profusely enough.

5

Decision of a Lifetime

I actually joined the Marines during my senior year in high school, but I had made the decision to join the year before, when I was seventeen years old. The stories that my father told me had made such a strong impression that joining the Marines was really the only plan I had. You could say that I was obsessed.

I was slight, only about 130 pounds, but athletic; in my senior year I ran every day after school to get ready. I knew I was going to join the Marine Corps, but I didn't tell a soul. I never told my parents, never told my friends. I figured I could get talked out of it if I did.

Friends can influence you, and I thought mine would say, "You're crazy. We're all going to college. You're out of your mind."

I would have gone to college if I hadn't enlisted in the Corps. My school was focused on academic achievement, so probably 95 percent of the students went on to college. In Long Island, the suburbs, we were all expected to graduate from high school and then go to college.

I waited until the night before my reporting date to inform my parents. They were shocked. I remember each day knowing that the reporting date was getting closer and closer, and that I had to tell them, but I couldn't. "I can't do it tonight. I can't do it tonight." Finally I didn't have a choice.

I said, "Ma, Dad, I got something to tell you. ..." They were lying in their bed watching TV, and I told them. They were stunned, but there was nothing they could do or say. The next day I left for boot camp.

I wasn't a bad kid, but I just had this gut feeling that I needed more discipline, and I wanted excitement and adventure. I was a senior in high school, so I was conscious of the war in Vietnam, but I wasn't concerned, and I knew nothing of the politics behind it all. As a student, it never dawned on me how many troops died, how many bombs were dropped, none of that.

My thoughts weren't all that patriotic then, like they are now. All I thought about was adventure and surviving boot camp. I almost forgot the part after that: we all go off to war. I wasn't scared about that part, just boot camp. I had heard about the Marine training camp at Parris Island in South Carolina, that it was tougher than tough.

I worried. Maybe I wouldn't be physically fit enough, mentally fit enough.

The recruiter had told me that I had to memorize eleven general orders. Each general order is like a paragraph long, and in those days you had to memorize them all. So that's what I did during my senior year, concentrated on memorizing the eleven general orders. Four months after I graduated I was off to boot camp. I had to report to Fort Hamilton in Brooklyn at 9:00 a.m. sharp. A relative who was in the Army drove me. He just dropped me off and said, "I'll see you in three years."

No big scenes. That was that.

6

Welcome to Parris Island

The bus ride to South Carolina felt adventurous. There were thirty to forty of us on the bus, a bunch of teenagers, seventeen, eighteen, and nineteen. No one knew each other, so we told each other where we were from: Somebody came from Albany, others from Staten Island, Brooklyn, the Bronx, Manhattan, north New Jersey, all the way up in Rochester. None of us knew what to expect.

We hit Parris Island at 2:30 in the morning, and the bus door opened and the drill instructor burst in screaming.

"What the fuck?!" he yelled. "Get the fuck off this bus! You got fucking ten seconds to get off this bus—and nine are gone!"

Pure culture shock. We stumbled all over each other.

At 2:30 in the morning, we couldn't see how drab Parris Island was, mostly just greens and grays, but we found out soon enough.

After they chased us off the bus, they gave us boxes. We had to strip to our underwear and put our "scummy" civilian clothes in the boxes to send home to our parents. "Scummy" was the drill instructors' term.

They overpower you with everything at boot camp. You are in such a whirlwind situation that it's like being thrown into a Nazi concentration camp. That's how overwhelming it is. Their objective is to tear you down to nothing, strip you of your civilian identity, and build a Marine.

It's like you're not a human anymore. They examine your body, and you're in your shorts—they call them skivvies—and you're standing in line and a man comes and paints numbers on everybody's chest: 1, 2, 3...12, 13. So I wasn't a human being. I was number 12. It said so on my chest. It's like you're totally stripped of anything to do with humanity.

You sit down and they grab you. "Next!" You're in line. "Next!" A drill instructor flings you on top of a garbage can, not a chair but an overturned metal garbage can. Then they cut off all your hair with electric clippers.

Zwoom! Zwoom! Zwoom! "Next!" Zwoom! Zwoom! Zwoom! "Next!"

Afterwards, they gave us soap, toothbrushes, that stuff, and we kept them in wooden footlockers with our other personal belongings.

While we were being processed, the base doctors asked medical questions of the whole group.

"Anyone who has allergies, step forward!"

"Who is on medication?! Step forward!"

"Anyone had a venereal disease?! Step forward!"

I stepped forward.

I caught gonorrhea from one of the maids in my neighborhood; when I was barely fifteen I had sex with several of them. But it caught up with me because I was in school one afternoon and went to piss, and it burned as if someone was shoving a knife in me. I managed to finish the day and make it home on the school bus, and in the middle of the afternoon, I went straight to bed.

My mother knew something was wrong, but I couldn't tell her what. Not my mother. No way.

"Ma, please call Dad. Just call Dad."

"What's the matter?"

"Just please call Dad."

She called my father at his store in Flushing, Queens, and he drove home. I told him that my penis hurt. But he didn't know anything about venereal diseases, and I never said anything like, "Dad, I got laid by the maid a few days ago, and now my penis hurts." He was clueless.

My father called the family doctor, Dr. Edelstein, and we met him at the brand new Syosset Hospital, which was only five minutes from my house. The doctor examined me and told my father, "Your son has to tell us who gave him gonorrhea. Some little girl in his school must also have gonorrhea, and we have to inform her parents."

I wasn't about to say that I caught it from one of the maids, and neither the doctor nor my father was that insistent, so I kept my lips zipped.

The doctor told my dad that his son was the very first venereal disease patient to be treated at Syosset Hospital. That didn't sit well with my dad.

But I had to tell the doctors at boot camp, so when they asked us as a group, I stepped forward. I was the only recruit who did. I wasn't embarrassed. I stood out there proud and thought to myself, "They're all virgins! It looks like I'm the only one who got laid." The drill instructors and doctors weren't as impressed as I was.

"Back in formation, maggot."

I felt cool, for all of five seconds.

We received our war gear and were fitted for uniforms and boots and issued belts and helmets, and it was probably 4:00 in the morning by the end of processing. I hit the bed thinking that I was going to sleep for the next five hours. Half an hour later—BOOM! —time to get up.

They threw the lights on and everybody had to jump out of their racks—that's what they called our bunk beds—and at exactly the same time, hit the deck and stand at attention in our underwear. If somebody was slow getting out, they yelled at us and everyone had to do it again until we all jumped out in sync.

It was so intense: up at 4:30 a.m., and probably when we hit the racks at 9:30 at night, it took all of three minutes to fall asleep. We were so exhausted from the physical strain of constantly running, jumping and climbing.

None of the training I did during my senior year of high school prepared me. I used to put on my nice sneakers and nice gym shorts, and then jog around nice and easy. Now I was jogging in combat boots with a cartridge belt, a pack on my back and an M14; instead of my nice shorts, little T-shirt and my sneakers, I was running and carrying forty pounds of war gear on me. Totally different.

7

The First Guy
to Die

The drill instructors yelled constantly. After two or three days, we were sleep deprived and our worlds were spinning.

They had us good then. They told us they were about to kill us for being dumbasses, and we believed them. We were so bewildered and isolated from the civilian world that it was easy to imagine them killing us and getting away with it.

"What did I get myself into?" I thought. "I can't believe I'm going to be suffering like this for the next three years."

A drill instructor was yelling at us, as usual. The rifle range was about two miles away, and we could hear these little pop-pop sounds: pop-pop, pop-pop, pop, pop, pop-pop.

"You hear that, you maggots?!" the drill instructor screamed.

That was what Marine Corps drill instructors usually called recruits. To them, we were "maggots," "fucksticks," "asswipes," and "ladies," never Marines. We were lucky when they called us recruits.

"Hear that, maggots?!"

"Yes sir!"

"Well, those are the recruits that can't make it," he bellowed. "You think we're sending you home to mommy and daddy? We are

31

not sending you home to them. We are killing you! Actually killing you!!"

Now instead of pop-pop, what I heard sounded like BOOM-BOOM! BOOM-BOOM! We maggots looked at each other thinking, "Holy shit! This is bad. This is really bad! They're killing us if we don't make it!"

The next day happened to be a Sunday. I had no idea. Every day is the same at boot camp. A Monday is a Tuesday is a Saturday or Sunday. Every day, up at 4:30, the same routine. Two or three days in, everything is upside down.

Our drill instructor stormed into the barracks screaming and ninety guys snapped to attention.

"I just know, I just fucking know, that I ain't got no Jews in my platoon!" he yelled. "I just fucking know that I ain't got no Jews in my platoon! If I do have a fucking Jew—and I know that I don't have a fucking Jew—take a step forward!"

I hoped that I wasn't the only Jew, and that at least one or two other guys would step forward.

Sure enough, I stepped forward and no one else moved. Not a soul. I stood there in front of ninety recruits.

"Oh fuck, here it comes," I thought. "Didn't even last three days."

Then the drill instructor asked *all* Jews to face left and march. Alone and obvious, I marched past him and down the length of the barracks, past all the other recruits. The door was open, and I could see three men in dark suits, guys in their forties and fifties. Undertakers, I figured.

My thoughts churned as I marched. I wasn't even a very good Jew.

For my Bar Mitzvah, I had to go to Hebrew school from age six to age thirteen. So when I was twelve, I kept failing and failing in Hebrew school. I was dumb in Hebrew. I couldn't learn it. I had a hard enough time with English, and then I had to learn to this stupid Hebrew stuff three days a week.

It was during the year before my Bar Mitzvah that my mother started panicking.

"You can't speak Hebrew! What are you going to do on Bar Mitzvah day?"

"No problem," my father said. "Get him a tutor."

So once or twice a week, a rabbi came to tutor me. I would go to my regular Hebrew classes, and then at night this jerky, old, big-bellied, bearded rabbi would come to tutor me. He'd show up right after dinner. I'd get home, do my homework, have dinner, and then this guy would arrive to try to teach me Hebrew. He was probably in his fifties, but he looked like he was in his nineties.

We lived in a typical Long Island house, three bedrooms upstairs, kitchen and living rooms downstairs. He would sit in a chair in my room, and I'd sit at my desk. He had no patience to really try to teach me Hebrew, so he would play a record of Hebrew words and phrases. It was always the same record, one he probably had made himself.

His neighbor must have had a dog when he made the recording because about two minutes into it, I could hear the dog howl. I learned zero Hebrew. What I did learn was to wait the two minutes until the dog howled, and by then he would be sound asleep.

He would come in, and my mother would be cleaning in the kitchen or something. He'd go to my room and shut the door, and she would be happy. My tutor was there to teach me Hebrew.

He and I didn't even talk. He put on the record; two minutes, the dog howled and he was out cold. I had it all down. I'd go, "One, two...," and that stupid dog would howl, and he was sound asleep. He would undo his belt after he sat down, and his big belly would hang out while he slept. It was so ridiculous. He was charging my parents for his nap time.

I finally told my mom. I told her to wait a few minutes and then come in. The guy was out cold. I howled like the dog when she came in, and this guy jumped ten feet in the air, scrambling all around.

He was gone after that and I had to say my Bar Mitzvah in English.

So marching from the boot camp barracks toward the men in dark suits—the undertakers—I thought that being Jewish was going to be a pretty stupid reason to die.

"I can't believe it. Here I didn't even tell my parents I was enlisting until a couple of nights ago, and now I'm gonna be the first guy in my boot camp platoon to die. I can't believe I'm the first guy. The Marines are gonna kill me. I'm the first guy they're going to kill."

The guys in suits could tell I was uneasy.

"Calm down. Calm down," they said. "We're civilians. We're from the B'nai B'rith. We know that you're Jewish. We're here to take you to Jewish services."

My first week in boot camp was such a blur that I didn't realize it was Sunday, and I still didn't believe them. "They're going to cart me to the firing range and they're going to kill me."

I swear, that's what I thought. My eyes were still bugging out.

"Calm down. Calm down," they said. "Every Sunday we come and look for new Jews, and you're a new Jewish recruit." I didn't know what day of week it was, and I had no idea the Corps made allowances for religious services for everyone, Catholic, Protestant, or Jewish, every Sunday.

I still didn't really believe them until they walked me to a little chapel and we went inside, and four other recruits were there. We weren't Marines, just recruits, and it was the first and last time that I had the opportunity to talk with other recruits.

There was no talking during boot camp. If we wanted to talk to another recruit about something, we had to ask the drill instructor for permission: "Sir, the private, Private Barry Fixler, would like to request permission to speak to…"

Then we would hear: "What the fuck do you want?! What the fuck does so-and-so have to say to you?! What the fuck?! Are you gay?! Are you both faggots?! Are you fags?!"

That's what we'd get. We might say, "No, sir! We want to talk about our M14s!"

It didn't matter. What we heard in response was something like, "Bullshit! You want to put the M14 up your ass, right?! You want to put it up so-and-so's ass! Isn't that right, private?!"

I never requested permission to speak. I spoke to nobody. I couldn't.

"What?! Are you both fags?!"

The B'nai B'rith people took a picture at the chapel that first Sunday of recruit training and sent it to my parents. My mother didn't show it to me until after I was home from Vietnam. The back of the picture said: "Best wishes B'nai B'rith Savannah, Georgia." So they came from Savannah to Parris Island just for the recruits.

It was nice of them, but I can never forget that day because all I had been thinking was that I was going to be the first guy to die.

8

Learning the
Hard Way

As recruits, we learned that everything in the Marine Corps has to be exactly so. The sheets on our racks had to be tight—tighter than tight—until we could bounce a quarter off of them. The drill instructors really would do that, bounce quarters.

In the beginning of recruit training, I would open my blanket and tuck myself in. I had it folded a certain way, tucked in nice and tight, but sleeping in it messed it all up.

It just didn't pay to slip underneath the blanket and ruin all the creases, so I slept on my back, on top of the blanket, so I could jump out and quickly pull it tight.

We had a few minutes before bed each night to take care of personal business. It wasn't free time that we could use to chat and hang out. We were ordered to write letters home, polish our brass and boots, or clean weapons. It was work, but it felt like rest.

Then a drill instructor would storm in.

"Ladies! Get your shit squared away and prepare to mount!"

We didn't get into bed; we mounted our racks. When we heard that order, we would quickly stow our gear in our wooden footlockers and then line up in front of our racks, always at attention.

"Ready, hoo-agghh!"

That was the order to mount, and we'd jump into our racks as quickly as possible. We were still at attention, but on our backs.

The drill instructor would pace through the barracks for a few minutes reminding us how we had screwed up during the day.

"Alright ladies, at ease!"

In unison, we'd chant our Marine Corps bedtime prayer: "Good night Chesty Puller, wherever you are."

Lights out. We'd fall asleep within minutes. There are no insomniacs in boot camp.

At night in boot camp when everybody was sleeping, one guy put on a cartridge belt and helmet and carried an empty rifle and walked guard duty for two hours, just in case of an emergency. It was called fire watch.

The drill instructors never left the platoon. They had a private room in the barracks and babysat the recruits, monitoring their every move. Fire watch was boring, up and down, up and down the aisles while everyone else slept.

We all had to do fire watch on a rotating basis, probably once a week. It really cut in to our rest, and we dreaded it.

The drill instructors had beautiful ice-cold water fountains right in the hallway near their quarters that we weren't allowed to touch.

The only water we were allowed to drink in our barracks came from the sink in the head. That's what they called the bathroom, the head. We had to cup the water in our hands to drink it. It was a crappy way to drink water and we could never really get enough. We were always a little thirsty.

Sooner or later, the temptation of that nice, cool water from the drill instructors' water fountain became too much for some poor recruits. About two o'clock one morning, a recruit on fire watch looked around and decided, "I'm the only one that's awake. Who would know?"

As soon as he went over and touched the spring button to trigger the water, an alarm went off like a school bell. RRRRRRRR!!!! RRRRRR!!!! It wouldn't stop.

The recruit shook the fountain trying to shut it off, but it was all rigged so that only a drill instructor could shut it off.

The drill instructor stormed out of his quarters and went berserk.

"What the fuck?! You stupid fuck! You're gonna get us all killed!"

We didn't realize it then, but everything they taught us as recruits would translate to a lifesaving discipline in the jungle of Vietnam.

And the Marine Corps does not tolerate fat people. No fat bodies allowed.

Someone who was a little overweight but could do all the push-ups and the running could hang in there. But a fat body who couldn't do fifty push-ups and ten pull-ups was pulled from the platoon, put back two weeks or a month and made to exercise until they got in shape. Then they were reassigned to another platoon, but could never outlive the fat body stigma.

We had a few fat bodies. They were a little overweight, but they hung in there and could handle the minimum physical training requirements.

During chow time, whether it was breakfast, lunch or dinner, we marched in to the mess hall with a drill instructor, totally silent, so silent that we could hear people eating.

We would get on the food line with our metal food trays held straight in front of us; the next guy moved, and the next guy moved, very machine-like. Recruits in the serving line slopped out the food from the other side: meat in one compartment on the tray, potatoes in another, vegetables, and then dessert. We had to eat everything on our trays; no leftovers allowed.

After I was in recruit training a few weeks and knew the routine, I saw that dessert was lemon meringue pie. I hate lemon meringue pie.

I saw the slop line recruit scooping up the lemon meringue pie and getting ready to flip it on my tray. I went "Mmmmm," not saying anything, but I caught his eyes and he held onto the pie and shooed me off. I skated, got off the line with no lemon meringue pie!

But my luck, I sat next to a fat body. Fat body had a big lemon meringue pie.

We had to eat fast. Fast, fast, fast! The drill instructor paced up and down while we shoveled food—shoveling, shoveling, shoveling.

But the drill instructor saw that fat body next to me with a big lemon meringue pie, and he went off on him.

"What the fuck?! You're a fat body! What are you, fucking nuts?! You're not eating that!"

He snatched up the fat body's lemon meringue pie with his bare hands. I didn't have one, and he saw that, so the drill instructor slapped the fat body's pie on my plate: more for the skinny runt. I had to eat it and not say a word.

The drill instructor would have gone ballistic if I'd said something. I would have been done, finished. I'd probably have had to go to "motivation platoon." That's never good.

Of all the luck! Out of the 300 recruits eating at the same time, at the most there were five fat bodies, and I sat next to a fat body who had lemon meringue pie.

The Corps not only controlled what food went in us, it controlled when it came out.

On the second day of boot camp they introduced us to "the head," which was nine sinks, nine showers and nine toilets. The toilets had no privacy partitions.

I grew up accustomed to having my own private bathroom and my own shower. Before boot camp, I probably never went to the bathroom without closing the door. In school, if I had to take an emergency crap in the bathroom, I could do it in private because even the school toilets had privacy stalls.

At Parris Island, there were just those nine toilet bowls lined up like soldiers. Drill instructors lined us up, ten recruits standing at attention in a line in front of each toilet.

"Ready, hoo-aghhh!"

That was the command to mount the toilet. Nine recruits would step forward, one from each line, mount their respective toilets, and attempt to defecate.

The drill instructors gave each recruit exactly one minute to complete the task.

We had to shit looking straight at the other Marines looking at us trying to shit. In reality, they weren't looking at us; they were staring straight ahead into space, still at attention. When it got down to ten seconds for us finish, the drill instructors started counting down.

"Ladies! You have nine seconds to squeeze off those turds! Cut that turd short and move it out!"

And we *had* to be finished. It wasn't like I could raise my hand and ask the drill instructor for another minute, please.

I thought, "How the hell can I crap with ninety guys watching me?"

During the day if we had to shit, we had the choice of crapping in our pants or holding it.

There was usually a head call in the morning, a head call after lunch and one after supper. And if we had to take an emergency head visit, we had to request permission from our drill instructors. If we stuttered, they started badgering us and we'd get all confused.

One time a guy sneaked into the head and secretly crapped, but

41

didn't want to make the flushing noise, so when the drill instructor saw the turd in the toilet, he summoned all of us recruits together and asked who did it.

The guilty recruit raised his hand and said, "Sir, that's Private Smith's turd."

The drill instructor went off.

"You used my fucking head without permission! You're going to get us all killed! Now I want you to fucking eat that turd!"

"Yes, sir!" the recruit said.

He didn't look very enthusiastic, but he bent down and began fishing for the turd with his bare hands. The drill instructor stopped him before he could get a good grip on it.

"Get the fuck out of here!" the instructor yelled.

I stood at attention thinking, "Holy crap! The Marines even take shitting seriously!"

9

It's a Bitch on
the Thumbs

We all went to war in Vietnam with M16 combat rifles, but we trained in boot camp with M14s. The M14 became part of us; we lived and breathed the M14 and felt it in our thumbs long after we had left it behind.

We knew everything about the M14. It has a wood stock and weighs eleven pounds. We would put the M14s down on our footlockers and close our eyes, or they'd blindfold us, and we had about two minutes to take them apart and then reassemble them. All of us could do it, every one of us.

Obstacle course, distances runs…everything we did, we did carrying those rifles. If we happened to drop our M14s and a drill instructor saw us, we were going to end up sleeping with the rifle right next us under the covers, our new girlfriend for the next week.

Dropping our rifles was unthinkable, and if an M14 had a little bit of rust, even a tiny bit of rust, that meant brig time and possibly having your graduation delayed. It never happened to anyone in my platoon, but that was the threat they held over us.

The point was: Become one with the rifle and one as a group of men.

During marching exercises on Parris Island, we trained with eighty to ninety men divided into three columns, and the drill instructor was always on our asses.

"Left, right, left, right, march!"

"Right oblique, left oblique, column to the left, column to the right!"

Back, forth, up, down, swing rifle to the left, swing rifle to the right, swing it up, pull it up, parade this, up, down, this.... We had to memorize all the commands.

Everything had to be in unison. Ninety guys had to do everything exactly at the same time without losing tempo. If one guy got out of step, say made a left shoulder turn instead of a right shoulder turn, the drill instructor went ballistic.

"What the fuck?! You out of your fucking mind, private?! Don't you know your left from your right?! You fucked up! You're gonna get us all killed in Vietnam!"

The drill instructors would get in our faces. They would go completely ballistic, and we had to be punished. And if one guy screwed up and had to be punished, that meant everyone screwed up and had to be punished, all ninety of us. That's the thing: They made us a team, every man accountable.

I would tell myself, "I don't want to be the guy to fuck up and make everyone take the pain," but someone usually did, and the drill instructor would lay it on us.

"You fucked up! You fucking turd! You fucking maggot! You fucksticks! You're all gonna die in Vietnam!"

We lived in a relatively nice barracks, but to the drill instructor, it was a "barn." We were "ladies" who lived in a barn, and screwing up on the parade deck would send the drill instructors out of their minds.

Marching required real concentration. Getting ninety guys to do anything completely in sync is tough, and sure as shit, somebody somewhere was bound to screw up, and the drill instructors would order everyone to a halt.

We had to stand at attention holding our M14s, and we had to hold them completely level. The rifles had to be absolutely parallel to the ground.

On order, we had to pull back the bolt on the rifle, and on another order, we had to release it, and there was the problem. To hold the rifle correctly, we had to place our thumbs in the path of the bolt, and when we released the bolt, it slammed into our thumbs. We had to remain at attention and not say a word, even though our brains screamed, "Aghhhhhhhhhhh," and our thumbs throbbed.

The drill instructor would order us to march again, and then someone else would screw up.

"You pieces of shit! You fucked up! Are you out of your fucking minds?! You're gonna get us all killed!"

Back to attention. Bolts slammed into our thumbs again. Thumb throbbed—bbbbb-boom, bbbbb-boom, bbbbb-boom. Both thumbs got it, depending on what we were doing at the time that someone made another mistake.

We returned to the barracks with swollen thumbs, and a corpsman came in with a paper clip and held it over a flame until it was red-hot. We couldn't ask any questions, couldn't say a word. We had no idea what he was doing.

"What the fuck is going on here?"

The corpsman told me to hold out a thumb, which was black and swollen. He jammed that hot paper clip into the nail and blood just spurted.

"Jesus fucking Christ!" I thought, but I couldn't say that.

At least I knew what to expect for the other thumb, and blood spewed. All of the other guys saw that happen to me and knew what was up. At least the pressure would be relieved.

Mike Ali, a buddy from boot camp and one of my best friends, lost a leg and an eye in Vietnam. About nine months into his tour of Vietnam, North Vietnamese Army (NVA) soldiers overran his position and dropped a grenade on him. He lost a leg, and his eye is gouged out. He has little pieces of shrapnel floating around in his body and probably had more than 2,000 stitches sewn into him.

My thumbs are great now; they recovered from boot camp and don't have a mark on them. Mike's thumbs never recovered. They've been ugly since boot camp, and when we get together now, we laugh about it.

"Thumbs, man, fucking thumbs!"

When people meet Mike, they say, "Yeah, Barry was right, your thumbs arc fucked up."

10

Marines at Last

Boot camp Graduation Day is a big day, a very, very big day. It's the day that families come for a parade for the 250 or so guys about to become Marines. When the drill instructors say, "Fall out, Marines," you *are* Marines. You have graduated boot camp, and then you walk leisurely for the first time in about nine weeks; you walk leisurely and kiss your parents, hug your parents, and can actually talk.

My mother has a big mouth, and my thumbs looked so fucked up, just ugly, ugly, ugly. So I remember cupping my hand so that my mother never saw my thumbs. We all kept our mangled thumbs hidden from our parents. The last thing I wanted to hear was my mother yelling, "What happened to your fingernails?!"

I was afraid that I wouldn't graduate from boot camp. I was nervous that my mother would say something wrong or that I wouldn't walk right or I wouldn't salute an officer. I kept looking for officers to salute. We all did. The janitor of the base probably drove in and had ten guys saluting him.

The drill instructors never let down their guard. They never said, "Good job, Private Barry Fixler. I'm proud of you."

What they did was—and it was the best thing—acknowledge us as we were boarding the bus to leave.

As we stood in line outside the bus, they told us, "Board the bus, Marines! Good luck!"

That was it, but they called us Marines.

"Oh my God!" I thought. "We are Marines!"

———

I learned early on about the respect that some people have for the Marines, even if I didn't take full advantage when it was given to me.

After boot camp we were sent to Camp Lejeune in North Carolina for combat training. After combat training, which lasted about six weeks, they gave us ten days off. They called it "leave." I went home on leave in the summer of 1967.

My father gathered about a dozen friends to take me out for dinner at the Playboy Club in Manhattan. His friends were all businessmen, all executive types in conservative suits and ties. They were fun guys, though, all gamblers at heart.

It was effectively my going-away dinner, and they sat us around a beautiful oval table in a special room at the Playboy Club. They drank scotch, and we all ordered steak. If you wanted to live the good life in those days, you couldn't get better than a nice, thick steak.

I savored the smell of the cooked steaks when the Playboy Bunny girls brought them out. Those cuts of beef looked awesome, each about two inches thick, and the girls placed one in front of everyone but me. I thought that was a little odd, but not a big deal. No one else started carving into his steak. They were waiting for me to get mine.

I admired their steaks—they looked and smelled delicious—and we waited and waited. Finally, two Bunnies brought out my steak, and it was twice the size of the others, about four inches thick!

"Holy shit!" I told myself. "Look at that steak! Oh my God!"

All of the guys cracked up laughing, toasting each other and, of course, toasting me. They clapped when I cut into the steak and we all had a great time laughing and talking. We didn't think about how bittersweet the night was for my father.

On one hand, he was enjoying the camaraderie with his friends and his son, but on the other, he knew he wouldn't see me for a year and a half, and maybe never again alive. I was, after all, going to war.

I don't remember what the guys had for dessert, but they intended for my after-meal treat to be a Playboy Bunny! They came and took me by my elbow and told me I could go into another room with one of the girls for some special attention.

I couldn't. "No, no, no," I protested.

"Pick any one; they're yours," one of the guys told me. They were cracking up laughing and loving every second of it. They really made me feel special, but I was too shy. I just couldn't do that sort of thing in front of my father and all of his friends. Had it been my buddies there, I would have been a goner! Forget about me for the next hour!

My father and his friends sensed it, how awkward I felt, and they just let it die there and the girls walked away. No one was offended. I wound up having strawberry shortcake for dessert instead, and we had coffee and tea and some more drinks. I had never had a four-inch steak in my life or been treated so royally. That was good enough for me.

The last stateside stop before Vietnam was California, and the reason why I'm not full of tattoos is because I ran around looking for girls.

Recruit training at Parris Island and combat training at Camp Lejeune in North Carolina took about six months. They made us disciplined Marines and then taught us how to fight. Then we went to Camp Pendleton in California for another four to six weeks of combat training.

We were with mostly the same 150 guys in our company at Camp Pendleton who we had been with in boot camp, and I got real comfortable. It was like high school. Not all of the guys were friends, but we all knew each other and could recognize the familiar faces.

What was nice about Camp Pendleton was, for the first time, we had weekends off. We had a little liberty. We trained Monday through Friday, and if everything worked out and we had the weekend off, we went to Oceanside. It was the first town south of the base, about forty miles north of San Diego.

So a bunch of the Marines would say, "Saturday morning let's go to Oceanside and get tattoos! USMC! Hoo-raa!"

I remember thinking, "Yeah, yeah, OK."

And the whole platoon got up and took a bus into Oceanside to get tattoos: USMC, the bulldog, this, that.

Oceanside, of course, is in Southern California and it was crawling with pretty women wearing nothing but bikinis and light summer dresses.

I was on the line to get a tattoo just like all of the other Marines, and we were about twenty, forty deep. And I was standing there thinking, "What am I, a moron? These pretty girls are all over the place, and I'm on line to get a tattoo with these knuckleheads?" So I left the line and went looking for girls.

But guys are proud of those tattoos. We were Marines and we were entitled. You can't get a Marine tattoo prior to boot camp. If you come into boot camp and you have "USMC" tattooed on you, brother, you're in trouble. They're going to put you through hell.

But when you make it, once you *are* a Marine, you want to

show it off. We didn't have any idea what we were about to be thrown into.

We were about to find out why the drill instructors were so passionate about discipline. "You maggots are gonna all die in Vietnam!" was no idle threat.

B'nai B'rith emissaries took this picture and sent it to my parents my first week in boot camp at Parris Island. I believed the drill instructor who told me they were going to take me out and kill me, and I thought that the B'nai B'rith men were undertakers.

I strike a Jack LaLanne pose in Mitch Sandman's back yard while exercising to prepare myself for boot camp during my senior year of high school.

Boot camp buddy Mike Ali, center, and a fellow Marine, right, pose with me while we're cleaning the barracks at Camp Geiger, North Carolina, where we were in combat training. My shirt is not squared away, so we must have been off duty.

Another recruit looks over my shoulder as I read a newspaper at Camp Geiger, N.C.

My boot camp buddy Mike Ali poses at the JFK airport
on our way to California and Camp Pendleton for more
combat training.

My sister, left, and my cousin pose with me on the day
that I graduated from high school.

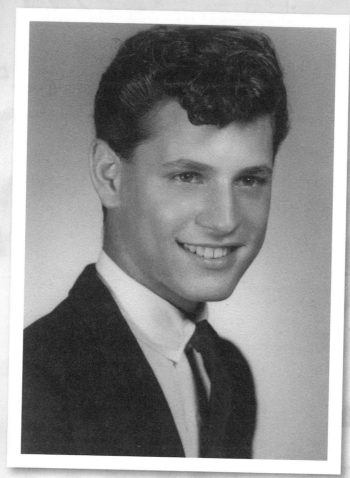

My senior year portrait from high school.

I lift weights in the back yard of Mitch Sandman's house in Long Island, New York. I was sixteen and preparing myself for the Marines.

I goof around with Mike Ali, left, at Camp Pendleton, California. Mike lost his thumbnails during boot camp.

Mitch Sandman, left, and me at Jones Beach, Long Island, New York. I'm on leave after boot camp. This was the last time I saw Mitch alive. The tattoo on his arm said "Born to raise hell."

I'm in the middle of a group of high school friends at Jones Beach, Long Island, New York, as we recreate the Marines' iconic raising of the U.S. flag at Iwo Jima during WWII. I had no idea then that I would soon be immersed in another legendary Marine Corps battle at Khe Sanh.

This is my photo from boot camp.

PLATOON 337 THIRD RECRUIT BATTALION
M.C.R.D. PARRIS ISLAND, SOUTH CAROLINA
SSGT. F.L. POLICE   SSGT. L.A. LEIST
SSGT. R.T. VANCE SSGT. G.M. WILSON
GRADUATED 28 MARCH 1967

INTO THE FIRE

11

'Fixler, You're Dead!'

The flights from Camp Pendleton to Okinawa and from Okinawa to Vietnam on civilian planes in a way symbolized our transition from civilians only a few months before to the warriors we were expected to become.

I felt I was at war as soon as I stepped foot on Vietnam.

"We're not joking around," I thought. "The fun and games are over. This is for real, and some of us are going to die."

Our time started when we landed in Vietnam, not when we hit Okinawa. We were obligated to thirteen months of combat for the Marine Corps.

"I'm fucking at war," I said to myself. "Oh shit, thirteen months of this. Thirteen long hard months."

The flight from Camp Pendleton to Okinawa was long. We all wore our day dress uniforms, and the stewardesses were all young and pretty, and I was thinking it was probably the last time I was going to see girls for a long time.

It was the middle of the night and we were sleeping, but I opened my eyes when this pretty stewardess walked past.

"Would you like some tea or some coffee?" she asked.

She was so pretty and I was so intimidated.

"Tea."

I only said yes because she was pretty. If she had been ugly or male, I'd have said no. I really wanted to sleep.

So she went and brought me hot tea: hot, hot, hot tea.

I really wasn't awake when she handed it to me, and the guy next to me shot straight up in the air. I'd dropped my hot tea straight on his lap.

"What the fuck?!" he screamed.

———

Everyone said Vietnam would be hot. The guys talked about it so often that I thought that when I got off the plane, my skin would boil.

I remember looking for the streets melting or something, like lava all over the place, going into hell. But it just felt like flying into New York on a hot July day: no big deal. But that was at the base in Da Nang. I learned all too soon that the jungle was a different story.

I was confident in my training, but on edge, definitely on edge.

"Will I be alive in thirteen months? How will I look? Will I have my arms and legs?"

We'd been briefed in Okinawa on our chances for survival: One-third of the guys would be killed; one-third would be seriously wounded; and one-third would return home fine.

In a way, I was anxious to at least get shot at and to shoot back. I wanted to get that over with.

We had trained as a group—150 of us—through boot camp at Parris Island, combat training at Camp Lejeune and Camp Pendleton and Okinawa. We were together the entire time.

"These are the guys I'm going to war with," I thought.

But I didn't realize that none of us were combat veterans, and the Corps wasn't about to send 150 green Marines to fight the enemy together. We wouldn't have known what the hell to do. We'd have been slaughtered.

I didn't think about that.

Instead, we were each going to replace Marines who had been killed or severely wounded, or those that were rotating out of Vietnam because they had survived their thirteen months at war. We were the replacements.

We landed in Da Nang and walked down the stairs from the plane to a Marine sergeant waiting on the tarmac. He started in alphabetical order, handing guys their orders telling them their assigned units.

"Okay, Adams? You're alive! Baker? You're dead! Crawford? You're a basket case!"

"Fixler?"

"Here sergeant!"

"You're dead!"

I'd been in Vietnam for an hour and the sergeant was telling me I'm already dead. I turned to Mike Ali, my good buddy from boot camp. "Fuck, I'm dead!"

"Yeah," Mike said. "Sergeant just told me I'm a basket case." We didn't realize at the time just how ominous that label was for him.

If you were alive, that meant your unit was in one of the less dangerous places in Vietnam. If you were a basket case, your unit was in a pretty bad place. If you were dead, that meant you were headed straight into the deep shit. Your unit was in the middle of the worst of the worst combat.

They didn't tell us that kind of stuff in boot camp. We trained and trained and were physically and mentally fit, but we were not combat veterans. Big difference.

We didn't think the dead/alive thing was funny.

The Marines who indoctrinated us in Da Nang led us around like sheep. We were all split up in a matter of minutes, and I started to feel deflated. We came in 150 strong, and now—boom, boom, boom— and I was uno, one person, confused, mind going a mile a minute.

"Get on that Jeep and the corporal will drive you to a helicopter. The helicopter will bring you out to your unit. You're going to Phu Bai."

No one explained anything.

I got on the Jeep. I climbed on the helicopter. The guys on the chopper already were in the war, seasoned, and I was new. They wouldn't have even given me the right time of day, and I didn't have the balls to ask. No one respected me.

The helicopter landed in Phu Bai, and I needed to report to division, report to regiment, report to this, report to that. I was with the 26th Marines; that was the regiment. The battalion was the 2nd Battalion.

"You're new here? You go over there. You have to go see the first sergeant."

The first sergeants then had fought in World War II and Korea and had no respect for the guys from Vietnam, none at all.

"My war was tougher than your war. Don't even tell me about Vietnam. We did Iwo Jima. We did Okinawa. We did the Chosin Reservoir." They had to have twenty years in the Corps to be first sergeants, so to them, compared with World War II and Korea, Vietnam was a joke.

I wasn't even a flea to those guys. I didn't know what was going to happen. I was confused, ready to fall apart, but I didn't show it. I had a presence about me always, but I was going to war, and I might as well have worn neon lights saying, "I HAVE NO COM-BAT EXPERIENCE!"

The first sergeant looked at my orders. "Get out of here and get your seven eighty-two gear!"

I didn't know what that meant, and it showed.

"That's your deuce gear! Get out of here!"

Damn, I didn't know what a deuce gear was, either, but I wasn't telling him that, so I left and found another guy my rank to ask.

"Oh, seven eighty-two, that's your deuce gear, your war gear. Go to supply. Over there, that's supply." The private pointed at a building with sandbag walls. All the buildings had sandbag walls.

We arrived in Vietnam with only our dress uniforms, basically, so they issued me my war gear—canteen, k-bar knife, helmet, ruck pack, flak jacket, and rifle—and I reported to Echo Company 2/26.

The barracks in Phu Bai were very crude, all wood, no toilets, and built by the Seabees—a special naval unit capable of building and fighting. We called the barracks "hooches," and each hooch housed about twenty Marines.

The only toilet was a fifty-five-gallon oil drum that was cut in half, and we just defecated into that. I didn't find out until later that an oil drum toilet was a luxury. Relieving ourselves in the bush was far more crude.

I had to wait around for my platoon to get back from a combat patrol. They came in at four or five o'clock in the afternoon looking tired, salty, and tough.

They had to eat, write letters, clean their weapons and get some sleep, and at 0600 form up in front of the hooch ready for another patrol. That was it; no time to run around or bullshit. Sleep was paramount.

But I had no idea what was going on.

"Where you from?"

"New York," I said.

"Ah, Walsh is from New York!"

"I'm from Long Island."

That was always the first thing, "Where you from?"

"You'll take Hayes' rack," they told me. "You're his replacement. He stepped on a Bouncing Betty two days ago. Both of his legs are gone."

"Shit! Fuck! I'm replacing a guy who just lost both legs?!"

I sucked all of this in, and the guys barely paid me attention. They were just so tired, taking off all their war gear, putting some chow down real quick, writing whatever letters they could before time to shut the lights off. We couldn't have lights after dark. We'd have been targets. And we always had to clean our weapons. The M16s were our lifelines.

My new platoon mates ate C-rations, canned food, and they threw the little tin cans all over the place when they finished. These were Marines from the field, and they couldn't have cared less about keeping the hooch clean. They were headed back out on another combat patrol first thing the next morning, and knew there were no guarantees that they would even make it back.

The other Marines stationed on the base were responsible for cleaning the hooches. Combat Marines in my unit called those rear echelon Marines "Office Pogues" or "Remington's Raiders," in reference to the Remington typewriters widely used by the military.

"Fuck them. They're losers. They have to clean this shit."

I wanted to ask a million questions, but I couldn't in that situation, so I went with the flow. By nine o'clock, everybody was sound asleep, and food cans were scattered all over the floor.

I couldn't sleep. I lay on my cot with my eyes open, still mentally severing myself from the 150 guys from training. Guys snored here and there, but otherwise it was totally silent.

Then I heard strange sounds, like thumping, and they kept growing louder, louder and louder. No lights were on in the hooch—this was a combat zone and lights were targets—but I could see shapes moving on the floor. Finally my eyes were able to make them out: rats! Hundreds of rats! I'm not kidding you. Rats flying over guys, on guys, up, down, sideways. Rats! After we shut the lights off, the rats went after the food scraps left in the C-ration cans.

The seasoned guys didn't give a flying fuck. They were combat veterans. They'd seen so many worse things that hundreds of rats were nothing to them.

They were probably thinking, "Please bite my toe! If you bite my toe, I can get out of going out in the field, and I'll catch up on some sleep. Give me an infection or something. I'll spend three or four days resting in the hospital."

They loved that shit. Sleep, I soon learned, was a precious commodity, and combat Marines were always deprived.

"Jesus Christ almighty!" I thought. "Fucking rats!"

I took my woolen blanket and threw it around me and went outside and tried to sleep on the steps of the hooch. But I couldn't sleep.

Boot camp had toughened me physically and mentally, but now here I was across an ocean… and clearly in over my head.

12

Welcome to
a Hot LZ

"Get the fuck up! Wake the fuck up! Saddle up!"

The corporal acting as platoon sergeant was barking out orders. We had to go out in the field to back up a platoon involved in a major firefight.

There is only one way to become a seasoned combat Marine, and that's to be thrown head first into the shit over and over again until you learn. I came as green and starched as my unsoiled war uniform, and that took some time to wear away.

I had my combat gear and my unit assignment; all I needed was combat experience. It was time to bust my cherry. No warm up period.

When a new guy came into Vietnam, they hooked him up with a seasoned guy. Then someone got killed or wounded and more new guys came and the process repeated itself.

Tom Eichler was my squad leader and one of my mentors. We called Tom "Ike," because his last name was Eichler, and he was hooked with me because I was green. Ike was a seasoned guy, already twenty-five, twenty-six years old. I was all of nineteen.

We formed up in front of the hooch with the rest of the platoon.

I was excited and clueless. Tom was cool, cool, cool. I was wide-eyed, watching everyone, listening to everything, trying to suck everything in.

I followed the platoon to the helicopter pad. There was a sense of urgency as we boarded the helicopters, and somehow Tom and I ended up on different birds.

We all wore war gear, and my heart pounded.

Guys started talking as we neared our landing zone.

"Pass the word, hot LZ! Hot LZ!"

"Hot LZ! Pass the word!"

"What the fuck's a hot LZ?" I thought, but I had no balls to ask anybody.

It turned out that an LZ was a landing zone, and a hot LZ meant that the enemy knew where we were going to land, that they were ready for us. Choppers landed for ten seconds, dumped their Marines and got the hell out of there. As soon as the Viet Cong knew where we landed, they hit us with mortars—short-range bombs that weigh about seven pounds—and rocket propelled grenades.

When Marines landed in a hot LZ, we had to be organized to run. We couldn't just go, "Aaahhhh!!!" and run for a tree or something.

I didn't realize that I already was carrying so many weapons: my M16, grenades, pop-ups, gas grenades. I carried a rocket launcher on my back, and each rocket for it weighed seven pounds.

Green privates were essentially mules. They carried ammunition for the machine gunners and rounds for the mortar guys as well. If we were carrying fifty pounds, they gave us another thirty pounds of somebody else's war gear to carry. The more shit we had in tow, the harder it was to walk in a jungle.

The helicopter was almost there, and the guys turned to me.

"Hey, you want a few more grenades?"

"Hey dude, carry this mortar round for me!"

"Hey, you want this? You want that?"

"Yeah, yeah," I answered, and all of the guys gave me some of their gear. Part of me wanted to prove that I was capable, and the extra gear also made me feel more powerful.

I weighed about 130 pounds, and I must've put one hundred more pounds of equipment on me. It felt OK when I was sitting, but I might as well have been carrying suitcases. My heart pounded.

The chopper touched down and we jumped out, all organized. I ran two, three steps and fell down flat on my face; I was loaded with too much gear.

The Viet Cong shot mortars and rockets at us, and a corporal had to run back and get me. He stood over me and screamed.

"You fucking idiot! You fucking piece of shit idiot!"

He took all that extra crap off me and threw it to other guys and we got out of there. The other guys were just pulling a goof.

War warps your sense of humor, and someone willing to be your mentor can help you survive.

"Skinny" was one of the first guys I bonded with in Vietnam. I regret that I don't remember his real name, but he was a thin guy, and we always called him Skinny.

Skinny was already seasoned when I hit Vietnam, but we took a liking to each other and he took me under his wing and kept an eye out for me even after he rotated back to the States. I can't remember his real name, but I'll never forget the man.

When you're in a squad with ten or twelve other guys, you naturally get friendly with each other, even though instinct tells you that the guy next to you may get killed tomorrow. You get friendly, and usually with one or two of the guys, you get really close. Skinny and I got close, pretty much from my first week in country.

Sometime around my first week in the jungle, we were sent out with another squad on a night ambush. Our job was to wait along a trail at some distance for the first squad to engage the enemy in a firefight and then light them up when they tried to run.

The first squad's job was to ambush them and force them to retreat toward our position, and then we were supposed to finish them off. A double ambush. I heard the explosion of gunfire when the enemy walked into the first squad's trap, then we braced ourselves and waited for them to come our way.

What I didn't know was that Skinny was watching me. Did I shake or grit my teeth or fumble around like some Gomer Pyle? Could the squad rely on me in a stressful combat situation? I was green, after all.

The first squad tore into the bad guys big time, and those that may have survived never did come our way, but Skinny saw something in me that he liked.

The next morning, after daybreak, Skinny turned to me and said, "Man, I'm impressed. You held your own." He didn't sense nervousness or fear from me that night while we waited for the enemy. After that, in his mind, I was one of the guys.

Skinny was almost a short-timer with only about four or five months left on his tour, and guys that were about to get out of Vietnam often didn't want to bond with new boots who still had a whole tour and a world of danger ahead of them, but that didn't stop Skinny. We liked each other and we hung out, grew really close.

Now Skinny was a New Yorker like me, but from Brooklyn or the Bronx. Still, when he rotated out in the winter, he promised me that he would contact my folks in Long Island and tell them, "Your son is a good Marine who's with a good group, and he will come home alive. Your son's sharp and he'll come home alive."

Marines only received a ten-day leave when they were first sent home from Vietnam, but sure enough, Skinny and a couple of New York guys that he was sent home with took one of their precious days to go out to Long Island, which was totally unfamiliar turf for them, to go see my parents.

He kept his promise, and my parents were very welcoming and grateful. So was I. It was a small act, but the meaning was huge.

No Marines in my squad were killed on my first patrol, and experience later taught me to appreciate such days.

That afternoon, we ended up at another landing zone and waited for choppers to retrieve us.

The LZ was a flat, open field with a tree line about one hundred yards away. There were about thirty of us, and we were a little early for the choppers. No bad guys around, and no incoming. The other guys seemed relaxed. Then I heard a popping noise.

"What's that?"

"We're being shot at," a guy said. "Probably some fucking old villager with a World War I, World War II rifle."

"You gotta be shitting me?" I thought. They could tell by the sound that it was an old rifle, and they weren't even flinching.

Pop. Pop. The shooting continued. Pop. Pop.

I was the only one jumping. No one else seemed to give a rat's ass about some old villager trying to kill us.

Finally, the rounds started coming too close to us, and the sergeant yelled out, "Who the fuck has a shotgun?!"

"I got one, Sarge," someone said.

"Shut that fucker up!"

This guy with the shotgun, he was a seasoned Marine. He walked straight toward the tree line where the bullets were coming from, and he screamed at the bushes.

"Fuck you! Fuck you!"

Then he emptied the shotgun: Ba-boom! Ba-boom!

I just sucked in all of it. I was so green.

"Holy shit!"

No more shooting came from the trees as he sauntered back, dangling the shotgun at his side.

"I shut him up."

13

Practical Lessons
in Discipline

The harsh training from boot camp had very practical applications in Vietnam, and the quicker that we learned, the better the chances were that we would live to see home.

Late fall in the United States is monsoon season in Vietnam. My tour began during monsoon season. We might see a couple of days of beautiful weather, and then a week straight of rain. It was a hardship. The Corps issued us these clumsy ponchos that we wore when rain fell, but the rest of the time we just used them as makeshift stretchers to carry dead or wounded men.

I wasn't seasoned yet. Everything was still new to me, and I was learning the ropes about everything. Boot camp is all about instilling procedure and discipline, and a number of times while I was learning how to be a Marine, I would ask myself, "Why all this harsh, harsh training of discipline, discipline, discipline?"

Stay still. Do not move, even if it hurts. Control yourself.

All through boot camp, we had to hold out our rifles and remain motionless for long periods of time. We were ordered to do fifty pushups and then another ten pushups and ten more pushups, and then stand in a frozen position.

Control yourself. Discipline, discipline, discipline.

I always wondered why, and I never put two and two together until the night of my first ambush.

It was early evening, and we were positioned along a trail that the Viet Cong used to ferry ammunition, food given to them by villagers and other supplies. Our location was great; we had a perfect line of fire.

Almost all of us wore our ponchos to fend off the heavy rain that patted the jungle leaves, making a static noise similar to the sound of television tuned to a station that was no longer broadcasting. Our ears tuned that out, and otherwise, everything was as quiet as could be.

We could see the Viet Cong fighters—gooks, we called them—making their way up the trail, and we were poised to make that night their last one.

But one of us made the slightest move to better position himself, and his poncho revealed us. It was the tiniest sound, just a faint rubbing, but it was enough, and the gook on point opened fire before we did.

We had an M60 set up, and the two Marines manning it ripped the enemy's point man to shreds, but he had given the other bad guys enough warning that they turned tail fast and disappeared back into the jungle, knowing that there was no way that we would chase them at night. We held our position until sunrise, when we confirmed that we had one kill, though we all agreed that it could have and should have been at least five.

We were bummed. It was such a small sound, just a faint little rub against a poncho, but their ears were so tuned in to the surroundings that it might as well have been a foghorn.

That was when I realized the reasoning behind all of that boot camp training about self-control.

Discipline, discipline, discipline. No exceptions, no excuses. Our lives depended on it. We learned a lot of practical lessons in our first few months as combat Marines, and if we were lucky, we lived to apply them.

I was still new and in the Phu Bai area, and my platoon was out in the field on patrol and had taken up a defensive position for the night.

Another group of Marines got into a firefight with the Viet Cong and radioed word to us that the gooks were running, and in our direction, so we tensed and waited for the bad guys.

We heard a noise coming toward us, and the Marine who was closest to it was so anxious that he stood up and just heaved a grenade in the direction of the sound. Then he stood there, I guess waiting to see gooks explode. It didn't register with him that you can only throw a grenade so far, maybe thirty or forty feet.

The grenade exploded, and the only person he saw get hit was himself. The blast peppered him with shrapnel, not enough to kill him, but enough to teach him a lesson. The gooks ran, and I made a mental note to myself not to do anything like that. At least I didn't learn that one the hard way.

14

Whatever It Takes

Ambushes usually ran from 6:00 at night to 6:00 in the morning. We stayed aware of each other, but we were quiet. We paired off, and each Marine took turns doing two hours of watch while his partner slept, and then they switched off.

During one of my early ambushes, we humped maybe 18 hours, and then only slept in shifts. My squad leader, Ike, relieved me and I tried to sleep, but I was new and too excited. I was maybe four to six feet from him, and I started to study him. His head would jerk every few seconds as he fought against exhaustion. He held two grenades, and I could tell that he was sort of nodding off.

"What is he doing?" I couldn't figure it out, so I crawled up next to him.

"Hey, what are you doing?"

"I have two live grenades here, and if I fucking fall asleep, we all die," he said. "That's the only fucking way I can stay awake."

Pull the pin from a grenade, and it's live. As long as you hold the spoon in, it won't go off, but if you let that spoon pop, you have about four seconds before the grenade explodes. If you release that spoon, you'd better fucking throw that grenade or run because it has kill radius of fifteen yards.

In combat, it's easy. Pull the pin, release the spoon and throw the grenade. But if you want to be cute, you can pull the pin and hold the spoon down indefinitely. Just don't release the spoon.

So what Ike did was pull the two pins, nice and easy, and hold the grenades with the spoons down. He just decided, "If I nod out, we're all dead."

That's what kept him awake, knowing that he had the responsibility.

"Oh fuck!" I thought. "He's my boss. I'm in a jam! He's nodding and I'm only a few feet from him. If he explodes, I'm dead too!"

I couldn't say what I thought, which was: "What the fuck?! Are you out of your fucking mind?! You're going to kill me along with you?! Kill your-fucking-self! You're not going to kill me!"

But I was a new guy. I had no clout. He was my boss.

I just waited for Tom to drop a grenade so that I could jump out of the way. Obviously, he didn't blow us up, but he rattled me good.

Six months later, I could've said, "You're out of your fucking mind! You're fucked up! Kill yourself! I don't give a shit! You're not going to kill me!"

But I was new. I couldn't say anything.

"Oh fuck," I thought. "Now I can't fall asleep."

I had my own trick for staying alert, and to me, it beat holding live grenades.

I would go through each individual in my family and think about how they might react to my death.

"What if I die tonight? How would my family react if tonight is the night that I die?"

I would start with my father, and then my mother, and then my sister. After that, I moved on to my extended family. I had seven uncles: my mother's three older brothers and my father's four brothers. All of them had known me since I was a baby, and I would consider their different personalities in thinking about how they might react.

"Uncle Eddie. He was a pretty good uncle. What would he say if he heard, 'Barry's dead. Barry was killed in Vietnam'? Would he be distraught, or would he say, 'Barry was a great kid and I love him, but he was a man and he died for his country, doing what he wanted to do'?"

Or would it be, "Oh my God, this is my brother-in-law's kid," and "How could this happen to my nephew?"

I would move down the line to all of my cousins, and then my neighbors, and even on to my classmates in high school. I did this all very deliberately, and I never made it through the whole list in one or even two nights.

I would play out the drama in my head, and it was almost like watching TV, and the hours on watch just flew by. That trick kept me awake, alert and alive.

"How would they react if tonight is the night that I die?"

15

Bad Acronyms and Dirty Details

Each day was a learning experience, and learning to relay messages was essential.

We moved cautiously out in the field on patrol, each Marine about eight to ten feet apart. That way, if somebody stepped on a booby trap, only one guy would get blown up instead of two or three. It also was good in case we were ambushed. If four or five guys were very close together, a machine gun could mow them all down.

In order to communicate with each other, we had to "pass the word," meaning relay messages quietly from man to man.

The first time I got information passed up through me, I didn't know what a KIA or a WIA was. KIA is Killed In Action and WIA is Wounded In Action.

The first time that I heard those terms, a guy behind me told me to pass up to a Second Lieutenant Jones that Squad 3 had two KIAs and two WIAs. What I told the next guy was, "Tell Second Lieutenant Jones that Squad 3 has two KBPs and two WWAs."

The word got passed on all screwed up, and when it reached the lieutenant, he was probably thinking, "What the fuck?"

I'd never heard those terms before. But those were things that you learned in the field, just like you learned that sometimes, it's just more prudent to keep your mouth shut.

Our platoon was held up on one patrol, which was bad. You couldn't stall in enemy territory.

A sergeant passed up the message, "What's the delay?"

What came back was, "Corpsman is afraid to go over the bridge."

A corpsman is a Navy medic assigned to a Marine infantry platoon.

The bridge was made out of bamboo, and only one man could walk it at a time. It was like an old rope bridge you expect to see in an Indiana Jones film.

You could not freeze at a bridge during a patrol. If it was there, you had to cross it. But the corpsman got there and looked down and froze.

When word got back to the sergeant, he lost his composure and took off after the corpsman.

"What the fuck! Corpsman doesn't want to cross the bridge?!"

The sergeant was going to kick his ass and the corpsman knew it because he could hear the cursing, so he zoomed across the bridge.

———

We were humping in the field, a platoon operation, thirty or forty guys, and it was hot and we each lugged forty to sixty pounds of war gear. We were in staggered formation, no talking. There could be ambushes during the day, but it was rare. Most of the firefights happened at night.

We had been humping for hours in the heat when my squad leader, Ike, stopped us for a break, and I needed to piss.

"Alright guys, take five, drink your canteen and stay in place!"

That meant that when we stopped, we stayed in formation and

faced outboard to watch for the enemy. We were on their turf. We could have a drink but take nothing for granted.

Everyone had to stay put but the squad leader. He could move. He was the man. I wasn't the man. I was just a peon, an Indian. I couldn't move. He was squad leader; he had clout. He could walk wherever he wanted, bullshit with another squad leader, bullshit with the sergeant, whatever.

Ike went to either talk strategy or flat out bullshit with another corporal or other squad leaders.

"Fuck, man, I gotta piss," I thought. "What a great time."

Everything looked clear, so I just edged away from my spot, still looking at it the whole time, making sure no one saw that I was out of formation.

I was pissing, not looking where I was pissing, looking at where I should be standing, pissing, eye balling around me to make sure no one saw, pissing.

I didn't want to hear: "What the fuck are you doing over there?! You belong over here!"

So I pissed and hurried back to my spot. Nobody saw me. Perfect.

The break ended and Ike came back from bullshitting and strategizing with the other squad leaders. He walked over and picked up his helmet. We couldn't take off our helmets. Squad leaders could. It was a pecking order thing.

Ike reached down for his helmet and went ape shit, fucking berserk!

"Who the fuck pissed in my helmet?!" he screamed. "WHO THE FUCK PISSED IN MY HELMET?!!"

Ike's helmet had landed upside down like a bowl when he dropped it, and I didn't see where it came to a rest. It was sitting there like a bowl, and I didn't pay attention to where I was pissing.

I watched everyone else and the spot where I was supposed to be standing, and I pissed right in his helmet. I practically filled it up.

Nobody saw me, and I knew no one had seen me because I was watching them the whole time, and those guys would have given me up in a heartbeat.

They'd have said, "Fuck, he did it! He fucking pissed in it!"

Ike kept yanking the helmet up and slamming it down, screaming the whole time.

"WHO THE FUCK PISSED IN MY HELMET?!!!!!!! WHO THE FUCK PISSED IN MY HELMET?!!!!!!!"

I didn't say a word, not a fucking word. I just stood there. I couldn't believe it. I wasn't watching and I pissed in the squad leader's helmet. Ike is still alive today and I see him for reunions. To this day, I still haven't told him that I pissed in his helmet.

He'd say, "You're the fucking one?!! After all these years?!!, You're the fucker that pissed in my helmet?!!!!!"

———

Green Marines, or "boots" as we called them, were easy to spot by the cleanliness of their uniforms. The more time we spent in combat, the dirtier and saltier and more crusted our uniforms became.

Out in the jungle, we wore the same clothes day in and day out, and I never wore socks or underwear because of the humidity and heat. They would literally rot away. We carried between forty and sixty pounds of gear each and sweated so much that our uniforms became crusted from dirt and the salt from our sweat. We felt like mules and smelled worse.

Maybe three or four times during my entire thirteen-month tour, we got lucky enough to take hot showers at a combat base. Out in the field, when we got the chance, we made a perimeter around a stream, did a 360 and faced outboard. Guys took off everything and jumped in a few at a time. We did it real quick. Nobody wanted to get attacked with their pants down.

Nothing was easy in the field. After humping all day long, we found places to sleep and dig in. We carried E-tools, which in military lingo were entrenching tools, or basically, collapsible folding shovels. Occasionally, we would come across another small Marine outpost that already was dug in, but that was like a gift and didn't happen often.

Dig in, set the ambush and then hump out the next morning. It was pretty much the same routine day after day.

Sometimes we would run out of water on a patrol. One time I was totally out of water, and it was a scorching hot day and we were humping hard and fast. I became so thirsty that it felt like my tongue was swelling.

Desperation was setting in, but we were in enemy territory and there was no way to stop. The outside temperature was probably well over one hundred degrees. But it wasn't like I could raise my hand and ask for a water break. And I'm sure all the other guys were out of water, too, or running low.

As we passed parallel to a rice paddy I decided to sink my canteen into the thick, leech-filled water. I did it quickly so no one would notice. I just bent down and sank the canteen into the mud and used my index finger to keep the leeches out.

I was able to get about a quarter of a canteen of that filthy rice paddy water and I gulped it down. About twenty minutes later— BOOM! —fireworks detonated in my stomach.

I had the worst cramps. I couldn't tell the squad leader that I had cramps, so I had only one option. I blew liquid out of my ass and marched on, coping best as I could with the pain in my stomach while the diarrhea ran down my legs and into my boots.

I had the enemy to worry about; I had to watch my flanks, and I couldn't moan or groan or go down. It wasn't funny. I had the worst cramps, and I couldn't stop the diarrhea. It felt like a knife ripping through my guts.

Finally, an hour or two later, we had to look to dig in for the night. We were still in enemy territory and open to attack. I was digging and my pants were soaking wet, and my ass and my legs were soaked.

"Fuck this," I decided.

I took off my pants and threw them in the dirt, and the dirt absorbed the liquid shit, so I flipped the pants over and it absorbed the other side. I had my top clothing on, but no pants.

I wasn't embarrassed. It was all guys. Had I been with a female, I would've thought twice about doing that, but my pants were fucked up with shit of the worst smell, and it wasn't even the smell that bothered me most. They were just soaking wet.

We were in combat mode—no talking—so no one could goof on me. The only ones talking were probably the squad leaders, discussing strategy.

It wasn't like back in the States, where you could joke around. It was wartime in enemy territory. Not one person even made a comment, and I wasn't embarrassed. I could have cared less. My pants were dry in half an hour.

16

Standards of Living

Whether you went to war or not, if you graduated boot camp and you love the Marine Corps, you're a great Marine; we're all on the same level. A Marine who earned the Medal of Honor and a Marine who just graduated boot camp merit the same respect: they are both Marines.

But most of the guys I served with were poor, and they were quick to notice the differences in our backgrounds.

My mother is a very gaudy person. My father, because he was a jeweler, had access to fine china and silverware and crystal chandeliers, and my mother liked beautiful paintings, so I grew up in a house that I considered very gaudy.

Around November of 1967, the guys in my platoon were relaxing in the safety of our hooches in Phu Bai when I received a bunch of pictures from home of my family celebrating Jewish holidays such as Rosh Hashanah and Yom Kippur.

The base at Phu Bai was relatively safe. We still ate C-rations, but it was very secure and we got hot food, too. The dozen or so of us in my platoon slept on cots that we kept our war gear underneath.

Occasionally we'd get a little free time for reading mail, and I was thumbing through the pictures my mother had sent. The family was gathered around the nice, long dinner table that came out for the holidays. The china, crystal glasses, the chandelier…that stuff didn't really register with me. All I really saw was my family.

The guys were lounging all around me, just eating and bullshitting.

"Hey, you guys, you want to see pictures of my family?" I said. "My mom just sent me pictures of my family."

"Sure!" they all answered, and everyone gathered over my shoulders.

I started pointing out people. "This is my sister, and that's my cousin, and…"

Then one of the guys piped up.

"Wow, Fixler, you are rich! Look everyone! Fixler is rich!"

I was taken aback, shocked. I never considered myself rich. I was a normal, middle-class kid who grew up in a typical house like you see on Long Island or here, where I live now, in Rockland County, New York. I wouldn't consider anybody around here rich. My parents were middle class; I'm middle class; everybody's middle class.

The guys didn't see it that way.

"You're rich! Oh my God! Hey, Fixler's rich!"

I looked at the pictures again, and then all the nice china and tableware stood out.

"No way, no way," I said. "Forget it. Forget it, man. I'm sorry. I'm sorry."

There was no way that the guys in my platoon came from homes that had long dining room tables, chandeliers, crystal and fine china. They just didn't.

"Fuck that shit, me being rich." I didn't want to be branded as rich. I thought it would have been a horrible thing. Who the hell wanted to be branded as rich?

"Bad move, Barry," I told myself. "Bad, bad move."

It's just like I wouldn't throw my combat experience at another

Marine who hadn't seen combat but was just as good a Marine as I was, or act like I was a notch above. I despise things like that. That's just not me.

When I first got into boot camp, about ninety of us were sitting around an instructor and he asked who had graduated college, and no hands went up. "Who attended college?" Maybe two hands went up.

"Who graduated high school?"

I had never known a soul who hadn't graduated high school. It was like eating, I thought, something that everyone just did.

I raised my hand, figuring that everybody would raise theirs, too. No. Out of ninety of us, only six to ten other guys raised their hands.

"Holy shit!" I thought, half pulling my hand down. "I can't believe this."

The instructor continued. "OK, who dropped out of high school?"

Then everyone's hands shot up.

"Wow," I thought. "What a learning experience."

———

Vietnam taught all of us, though, just how well off we are in America, and what a great country we have. It made me the patriot that I am today, and I may have first realized my devotion to this country on the day when I saw a simple gesture from a Vietnamese baby.

I used to like riding on convoys. Not that they were safer; it was just that we didn't have to hump gear, so for that reason, they were great.

I used to watch the vehicles in front of us to see what parts of the roads they used, and I would cringe when a driver of our truck would deviate from the tire tracks of the vehicle in front of us.

If it looked to me like we were going to veer out of the forward truck's path by even an inch, I would think, "Uh-oh," and I would cringe and sort of brace myself, expecting an explosion. It was probably like what our Marines face now in Iraq and Afghanistan: roadside bombs and improvised explosive devices. We just called them land mines.

One day we were on a huge operation and were going from Phu Bai all the way north to Hue City. It was a pretty serious mission, 100 percent on alert, all of us ready to pull our triggers if anything happened. It was so easy to get ambushed.

The drive lasted three or four hours and passed through dozens of villages, stop-and-go the whole way.

In each village, children came out and chased us, begging us to throw cans of C-rations to them, but what they wanted most was candy.

"G.I.! G.I.! G.I.!" they screamed, hands held out.

People may have heard rare stories about American soldiers killing or assaulting Vietnamese civilians, but I never saw anything like that. Never. If anything, we Marines went out of our way to do kind things. Good Marines are proud and have a natural instinct to protect, and children bring that instinct out even stronger.

We carried little Hershey's bars to throw to the Vietnamese kids. They loved it, and all of us enjoyed doing that for them. We didn't have much candy with us on the Hue City mission, and in each village, maybe twenty kids came running parallel to the convoy, ten on each side, with their hands out. Only one or two out of the twenty would get candy because that was all that we had.

"G.I.! G.I.! G.I.! American Number One! American Number One!"

As we slowed to a stop in one village, I looked down and saw a young kid carrying a baby that probably was only ten or eleven months old. The kid stopped and set the baby on a large rock beside the road so that he could approach us for candy.

The baby was too young to walk and just lay there on its belly. As I was studying it, the baby stuck out its hand like the older children.

"Oh my God," I thought. "This baby can't even walk yet, but it already knows how to beg."

For some reason that image of the begging baby embedded in my brain: The infant knew how to beg before it knew how to walk.

Someone could have shot at me and I wouldn't even have been able to react, I was so engrossed in that thought: The child couldn't even walk yet, but already knew how to beg.

That summed up Vietnam. The country wasn't poor, it was starving.

It was a reality check, a lesson to a nineteen-year-old Marine about how cruel life can be, and it made me very sad. That child grew up thinking that food, or things such as candy that passed for food, didn't come from its parents, it came from G.I.s.

But it made me think about how great America is and how lucky we are. Ninety-nine percent of the people in America have never experienced anything like that... and never will. It made me want to do something so that children wouldn't have to experience anything like that again. Not children.

It was a powerful image and a significant moment in my life. I've had only a handful of experiences in my life that hit as hard. Like when that thug came into my store and put the gun in my face to rob me. Time stopped, and my brain processed everything instantly: "This is the real deal."

17

'This is the Real Deal'

"This is the real deal. I HAVE to kill these two guys."

It is amazing how quickly the brain can work under stress. Three thoughts darted through mine on Valentine's Day morning, 2005: "This is the real deal; this is an automatic pistol, which I do not like;" and, "I HAVE to kill these two guys."

I slapped the gun away from my face. I only know from watching the store videotape later that I used my left hand. I had no time to contemplate; I reacted.

I'm a jeweler, like my father. I keep guns in my store. Bad guys with bad ideas rob jewelry stores, as he knew, and I am prepared in case they try mine. My store was prepared that day when those two guys came, and thankfully, so was I. I didn't know it at the time, but they had a body bag waiting for me in the getaway car.

I knocked the gun out of my face, ducked behind the counter and lunged the six feet to where I kept one of my pistols, which was holstered under the counter about eighteen inches above the floor.

I had to concentrate, do everything right. My life was at stake.

"Barry, you have to do this perfect. Snap open the holster. Use two hands. Pull out the pistol. Come up killing. … Come up killing."

The two robbers followed my movements as I dove under and around the counter. My brain registered: "One exactly parallel; one to my right."

I was so anxious to get my holster away from my gun that I flung it like a Frisbee, and it bounced off of the wall and next to my safe. Detectives who watched the videotape said that the flying holster distracted the crooks for a split second, and that was the advantage that I needed. I sprang up blasting.

I knew better than to stand still. That guy with the automatic locked eyes with me, and we tried to shoot off each other's faces, but both overshot.

I immediately went from defensive to offensive. I let go two rounds, and in my brain, the first guy was dead. Next jerk. I moved to my right and shot the guy in the white in the chest. Both of them went down.

The robber in black was stunned, but to my surprise he shook it off and popped up and ran for the door. I found out later that he wore a bulletproof vest under his trench coat, but the force of my round was enough to knock him down. The guy in white tried to crawl to his feet and run, but he wore no vest. My bullet was in him.

The front door glass of the store shattered from one shot, and the one in black raced out while his partner collapsed near the door and tried to drag himself away.

I kept my cool. I maintained self-control. I acted like the Marine that I am.

"Don't shoot, Barry!" I told myself. "Don't shoot! You're on the offense; you just won! Don't shoot again, Barry! They're running! DO NOT SHOOT! You won!"

I had no intention of shooting them in their backs, but I also had no intention of dying. For all I knew, they would regroup outside and come back to get me. I only had two rounds left and didn't want to be cornered in the store, so I moved toward the front door in a military shooting stance. If there were going to be another shootout, I wanted it to be outside. I wanted to control the situation and keep them on the defensive.

In reality, I had no rounds left. My brain counted three shots, but I had really fired all five rounds.

From the storefront, I saw a brown minivan scream past in the parking lot. I looked for a front license plate, but it had none. I did see the eyes of the driver, and it gave me great satisfaction. His eyes were about three inches wide, and the look on his face said, "What the fuck just happened?!"

Two of my fellow business owners in our shopping center were opening their stores at precisely that moment and saw the brown minivan speed away, just like I did. They called 9-1-1 within thirty seconds of each other and gave descriptions of the getaway vehicle.

The guy in the black trench coat who had shoved an automatic pistol in my face was gone, and his accomplice in white was face down in the doorway, half in my store and half out. One of my shots had felled him, and that was as far as he made it trying to get away.

"Don't let this guy crawl out," I told myself. "I don't want the cops to think I shot him in the street."

I totally forgot that I had everything on tape.

I kept my gun trained on the guy.

"Don't move! Don't you fucking move!"

I looked around for help, not knowing that the owners of other stores were dialing 9-1-1 at that moment, and I saw a woman jogger and yelled for her to call the cops, but she ignored me.

"Who the fuck are you?!" I yelled at the back of the bad guy's head. "Who the fuck are you?!"

I had the situation well in hand, so I wasn't panicked or scared. I was more pissed than anything, and I vented on the guy.

"Who the fuck are you?! You think you're good enough to rob me?!"

I never hit, kicked or so much as even touched him, and the police respected that.

Yell and curse at him? Hell yes, I did.

"You think you guys are good enough to get over on me?! Who the fuck do you think you are?! You think that you can rob me?"

I do have to tell the truth. I was on an extreme adrenaline high, and in the back of my mind, I thought, "Fuck, man, this is cool! I fucking love this that somebody tried to rob me and I fucking won! I just fucking love this! This is cool!"

When the police came, I had to downplay things and act regretful about the whole situation because I wanted the cops on my side. I couldn't be cocky or show the wrong attitude. I didn't want the cops thinking, "What, do you just go around shooting people?"

Then again, anyone who really knew me could've told them that I have a much longer history of people shooting at me.

18

Nervous Meal, Doomed Bridge

When we were ordered to guard a bridge in the Phu Bai area that wasn't very strategic for us, the way I saw it, my job was to throw grenades in the water and not get killed by villagers who we hoped were friendly.

Villagers used the bridge to get back and forth, and we were guarding it more for them than for the U.S. military. But it was a nice bridge—steel, not bamboo—that you could drive a truck across, and my platoon was given orders to protect it 24/7 for a week.

We knew absolutely and positively that either the NVA or the Viet Cong wanted to knock down the bridge, but for us, it was pretty easy duty. We had thirty or forty guys and just took turns on duty and off duty guarding the bridge.

It beat humping twenty or thirty miles a day in the field constantly on the lookout for booby traps and ambushes. We weren't going to step on anything that would explode, and the odds were less that we would be used for target practice. It was pretty nice, a relatively comfortable assignment.

The bridge was the most modern thing about the village, and the first thing we had to do was set up a perimeter and then establish the best place for guys in our squad to sleep when they weren't on watch. The shifts were two hours on, two hours off, two on, two off. We also needed the spot to stash our packs, ammo and C-rations, and just to chill.

Ike, our squad leader, found what looked like a great area with shade right next to a hooch, but an old lady stormed out of it scolding us.

"No, no, no, no, no, no, no!"

"What the fuck, no?"

"No, no, no, no, no, no, no!"

We could tell she was flipping out, but we didn't understand what she was trying to tell us. "Fuck her," we told ourselves, and we went about our business. But she knew how to make her point.

"No, no, no, no! Woo, woo, woo, woo, woo! Sssssshhhhhhhhh! Sssssshhhhhhhhhh!" She wrinkled her nose, but about then our own noses caught up with her message.

We were about to move into the village's public shithole, the public head. We found another spot quick.

We got friendly with the villagers in short time and gave the kids candy and things like that. One of the villagers must have taken a liking to me. By evaluating his hut and his demeanor, I could tell that he held some sort of authority in the village, and he must have seen me with the children and thought that I was a pretty easy-going Marine, or just naïve.

He approached me and in very crude English asked if I would have dinner with him and his family. I felt honored, so I said yes. It wasn't like I would be walking away from my duties. I would be right there in the village.

I told Tom, and he didn't give a shit.

"You gotta have dinner, fucking have dinner. We'll see you!"

He liked things a little risky, and to him it was just a joke.

"If they feed you a razor blade, we'll know this is not a friendly village."

That was the thing. We all had heard stories about kids giving Marines Coca-Cola with razor blades in it, and the Marines sucking the razor blades into their throats and bleeding to death. We'd heard about Vietnamese giving Marines hot tea laced with acid.

So I was on edge when I arrived at the hut that evening for dinner, and I didn't know what to do with my M16. The villager offered nicely to let me prop it by the door, but I politely said, "No way."

I thought, "Could he lunge for it and get me? Who would be closer to it, me or him?" I imagined several possibilities, none of which were good for me. The man was friendly, kids were playing with me, and his wife scurried around saying "Thank you" more times than I could count, but I thought of them as if they were snakes. A snake is good, good, good, indifferent, and all of a sudden it will turn on you.

I was suspicious of the tea, so at first I just dipped the tip of my tongue into it. I half expected my tongue to evaporate, just vanish right out of my throat.

I tried to act as sociable as possible, but all of these thoughts ran through my head: "Will the food be poisoned? What if I get cramps? I'll know they poisoned me, right?"

I only ate a little food, and the family kept giving me funny looks. They had no idea what was going through my brain. They must have thought, "Wow, this American is one fucked up guy. He eats slowly; he drinks with his tongue like a dog. He's licking the bowl!"

The whole time, I thought, "Barry, you're in a jam now. You gotta be careful. You wanted to be friendly with this family, and now you gotta lick your bowl so that these people don't kill you."

I had propped my M16 against the table, just out of my reach, and I kept thinking, "Who could lunge for the rifle quicker, him or me? What did I get myself into? Can you imagine if he somehow gets up in front of everybody and shoots me? What a way to go!"

I was under pressure. Are you kidding me? From acid, to razor blades, to everything that I could think of, to him shooting me with my own rifle because he said, "No, put it over there, put it over there." The mother could pick up my M16 real quick and throw it to the father so that he could shoot me. At that point, anything seemed possible.

Seasoning taught me to evaluate situations and make decisions. I decided from that point on that I would never let my M16 out of my reach again.

But the dinner worked out fine, and I was just healthily paranoid.

Guarding the bridge didn't turn out quite so well.

We figured that the enemy planned to sneak in from the water and attach explosives to the bridge to knock it down. So our jobs were to take grenades and throw them in the water every fifteen minutes so that they would explode and kill anyone trying to attack the bridge from below.

What was nice about it when it was my turn on duty was that I wasn't carrying or throwing my own grenades. If they had been mine, I wouldn't have wanted to throw them because then I would've spent my personal supply. We kept a whole box of the things—sort of community grenades—at the ready on the bridge.

My first time on bridge duty, I really had no idea what I was doing. I relieved another Marine around midnight and found myself with only an ARVN for company. ARVN (Army of the Republic of Vietnam) troops were South Vietnamese military reservists, and we were guarding the bridge because they couldn't hold it in the first place. They were our allies, but they were basically worthless. It was like us fighting with the Iraqi army. They were jokes, definitely not Marines.

So I relieved my fellow Marine thinking, "No big deal," but the last time I had thrown a grenade was in boot camp. I never had the opportunity to throw a live grenade other than in practice.

I picked up my first grenade thinking, "Fuck, man, I forget. How long is the fuse on a grenade? How fast will this explode?"

Would it explode in the air? Deep under water? Would I accidentally blow up the bridge?

My Vietnamese companion became really scared when I grabbed that first grenade, and that made me even more nervous. I pulled the pin, tossed the grenade under the bridge, and took off running. The ARVN did the same thing. I jumped, and he jumped along with me.

The water was right there in front of us. I was afraid I might take out the bridge or something.

"Fuck, man, maybe the ARVN knows what he's doing," I told myself. I didn't know what I was doing, that was for sure.

The grenade created a big bubble in the water when it detonated, like a huge fart in a giant bathtub.

"Whew! That was easy enough."

By the end of the first hour, we were both totally relaxed about it. I threw the grenades at will. They weren't my grenades, and they were plentiful.

I was off duty and asleep the next day when the enemy blew down the bridge. The Marine on watch was injured, and one of our helicopters lifted him out of there.

That was the end of our bridge guarding. We had nothing left to guard. The enemy just blew the bridge and disappeared into the night. We didn't take it personally, like we would have about a bridge that was strategic for the Marines.

Our attitude was, "Fuck it; it's a fucking village bridge. Let's move on."

19

The War Walks
Into a Temple

No official rite of passage existed for completing the metamorphosis from green to seasoned Marine. We had to learn the sounds of the jungle and the tactics of the enemy, and we had to learn to be composed enough under fire to apply our training.

I realized that I had become a seasoned combat veteran after three or four months in Vietnam, when one of the Jewish holidays came up.

My lieutenant, the platoon commander, came over and said: "Fixler, you're in country three or four months; you're entitled to an in-country R&R (rest and recuperation or recreation), and they say that in Da Nang they have some kind of Jewish services. You rate two nights, three days of in-country R&R. Do you want to go to these Jewish services?"

"Yes sir!"

I'm more spiritual than religious, and I knew it wouldn't be the best rest and recuperation, but it was a novelty.

"I'll do it, sir."

Traveling south to Da Nang took nearly a whole day.

I took a helicopter first, but it didn't exactly get me there. The crew just took me where they were going, and I had to keep catching rides on the ground from there.

I ended up on a cattle car, which is a huge troop transport capable of carrying about one hundred men. It looks like an eighteen-wheel tractor-trailer. The driver and another guy sat in the cab, and the transport was going from one side of the base to the other.

The truck had a slide on one side, so guys could board while it moved. Another Marine and I jumped on as it slowed, and we headed down a bumpy dirt road.

We only had to go maybe four or five miles, and by the time we came up on an Army soldier looking to hitch a ride, the driver had picked up some speed.

"C'mon! C'mon!" I told the guy, and he started running parallel to the truck. We were going about twenty miles an hour, and that was too fast. I put out my hand and the hitcher jumped, but he just missed.

One of his legs caught in the wheels as he fell, and we heard him scream. His leg snapped clean off, right above the boot. I know. We found the foot.

The driver didn't see it happen. We had to keep yelling and banging against the back of the cab to get him to stop.

Me and the other guys—Marines, Army—jumped out and went to help the poor guy. We put a tourniquet on his leg, and lucky for him, we were near a little medical compound, not out in the field, where it would have taken longer to get medical help. I'm guessing that he lived.

That's the way it went. We were young, mostly in our teens and early twenties, and we did things like that. Stupid accident. I think they classify those types of injuries as "misadventure" in the casualty reports.

I still felt bad for the guy when I got to Da Nang. I still wore forty, fifty pounds of war gear: my M16, about two hundred rounds of ammunition, my grenades, everything.

Da Nang had only been a short pit stop—a blur—when I first got to Vietnam, and after that, all that I saw for three or four months was jungle. My return shocked me. "Am I still in Vietnam?"

I never had an idea that the main base in Da Nang was so secure. People from the Air Force, the Navy, and the Army walked around without side arms, just like civilians. And civilians, Vietnamese, were all over the place: laundry people, that sort of thing. There were brick buildings, hot showers, air conditioning, and movie theaters. It all seemed unreal.

I found my way to the chapel. It was little, but it did the job: rows of pews, a wooden floor and a wooden frame. Crude, but not bad. Jews, Catholics, Protestants, everyone went there. The Jewish service already had started, officers only.

The Jewish officers were probably Navy surgeons, eye doctors, and dentists, about twenty of them, all in their dress white uniforms just like back in America. I walked in still wearing all of my war gear. I had a good month, month and a half of crud on me, but none of us in the field could smell each other because we all smelled that way. You can imagine how I must've stunk. I made a clunking sound walking across the wooden floor.

The rabbi saw me and his face froze; all of the officers turned around in their pews and looked, probably thinking, "Who the hell is this guy?"

The rabbi half stuttered. "A-a-are you Jewish?"

"Yes, rabbi," I said, backpedaling toward the door and suddenly feeling totally out of place.

"Officer Country," I thought. "Wrong place. Fucked up."

"You're Jewish?"

"Yes, rabbi."

"Don't go. You're here for the services?"

"Yes, rabbi."

It took him a little bit to regain his composure.

"OK. Please come in."

The officers still stared at me.

"Will you please put your gun outside the building?"

I'd been in the jungle for three or four months. The M16 was my lifeline, like oxygen. We never lost touch with our M16s the field. If you had to piss, you put it on your thigh. Pissing, shitting, or sleeping, out in the field we always had a grip on our M16s. Those weapons were our lives.

I had learned my lesson about parting with my M16 during that nervous meal with the Vietnamese family.

"Rabbi, I can't put down my weapon, sir. I'll just leave."

I could see all the officers still staring at my rifle, and then everything else: helmet, cartridge belt, grenades, gas mask, gas grenades. I walked in to the religious service straight from the war, extra salty.

"It's OK. It's OK," the rabbi said. He was about ten feet from me. "You do what's comfortable for you."

The rabbi wasn't comfortable. He stared at my M16 throughout the service. It was as if he suddenly realized that a real war surrounded him. I just sat there, a seasoned warrior in salty combat fatigues surrounded by kempt Navy officers in white dress uniforms. I felt as out of place as I looked.

The rabbi came up to me right after the service.

"I apologize to you. You have to understand that I just flew in to Vietnam for services and I never met an Army fighting man before."

He was a civilian rabbi and didn't know Marines from Army. I didn't correct him. He was just there for the officers. It was as if he didn't know that enlisted men who were Jewish existed. He probably thought that if you were a Jew, you were an officer. I could see the confusion on his face.

He seemed to want to know my name, but he knew I was going back out in the field, and he didn't know how to react. He was young, probably had not been a rabbi very long, and I could see that he was rethinking the idea of getting to know me any better.

He probably thought, "Why should I ask him his name? What happens if he dies? I don't want to know if he dies. If I keep in touch with him and he dies, I'm going to be devastated."

I left without him asking.

———

My hard-earned experience and my Jewish roots combined to pay dividends on an operation that dragged on days longer than we had expected. Nobody brought enough food.

Echo Company received orders to hump from our base in Phu Bai to a mountaintop deep in enemy territory. Company-sized operations were rare, and our commanding officer, Captain Earle Breeding, was with us. COs didn't participate in normal operations such as ambushes or patrols, so we knew it was something big.

The mountaintop took a full day to reach, and what we saw after we scrambled up the steep, rocky, tree-covered slope was nothing short of a catastrophe. A U.S. plane had been shot down, and debris and body parts were strewn all over.

No one survived. Not one body was intact. We saw boots with parts of legs still in them, horrible things, but we had a job to do, and we did it.

Our squad leader just told us to take enough food and ammunition for three days. To me, it was just another operation, another day of facing the enemy in their territory. We didn't ask, "Where are we going?"

But telling us to pack food for three days meant the mission was important, and the Jew in me told me to take more, just one extra can. Now, anything extra you took just made your pack heavier. A one-day supply of C-rations weighed about five pounds. So most guys only packed enough for three days.

In fact, I usually just carried enough for two or three and I was OK. This time, though, Jew Barry decided to bring extra.

When we went on missions that lasted more than three days, we usually found another Marine outpost where we could restock on ammunition and food.

But this mountain wasn't near any outposts, and climbing it wasn't easy. It was steep and covered with trees and rocks, and we had to ascend a single, crude path that Marines on point had cut with machetes through the heavy jungle foliage.

The climb took all day. Besides being extremely difficult terrain, the mountain belonged to the enemy, and we had to be careful. The enemy could have been hiding anywhere waiting to ambush us.

We had to climb the mountain ASAP, so we stuck to the single trail instead of keeping spread out. It left us vulnerable to ambush, which made it clear that the mission was important.

We could have been diced to pieces on a clear path. That was just the way the enemy did it. In addition to carrying all of our food and gear, we had to be ready to fire our M16s at all times, even when we were holding onto branches just to keep from falling off the mountain.

It's easier if you have two free hands, but we were carrying our M16s and our gear. I had a rocket launcher, too, and two rockets, plus my ammo and war gear and chow.

Reaching the mountain plateau took a full day, and you never want to see what we saw when we reached the top: total death and destruction, and the dead were our guys.

It didn't look as if the plane crashed into the mountain, more like it exploded above it. Trees were peeled back, but there was no main, bare, crash spot.

Our mission was to search for survivors, and then guard the site while the crash was investigated. It was immediately clear that no one had survived. It was as if you just took everything, shredded it, tossed it in the air and let it fall. Parts of plane and people were scattered everywhere. Nothing was intact.

Body parts were wrapped around trees. The carnage was all around us and the human remains were impossible to identify. We didn't even see dog tags.

As Day One dragged into Day Two and Day Three, it became clear that nothing was salvageable. Pieces of flesh were no bigger than a few inches. We couldn't even gather them after a couple of days because they became like Jell-O, decomposed. The flesh just became part of the earth. I don't remember an overwhelming smell of death because everything stunk: the dead and us.

Maybe my brain has blocked it out. I had seen death three days into Vietnam, and from that point, it became routine. Dead enemy was a good thing. Looking at enemy bodies was thrilling; they were like trophies. It was cool.

But these were dead Americans, and I didn't want to look. Some of the guys exclaimed, "Did you see the foot in a boot? Did you see that?"

I had seen an American foot in a boot on my way to Jewish services in Da Nang a few weeks earlier. That was enough.

"No, I'm not going to look," I thought. "Everybody's dead; nothing to bring back, nothing to bring back...."

Early on, a day or two into the mission, a helicopter tilted and hit a tree stump or something and crashed. No one was hurt, but no place was clear for the choppers to land after that. We lost our air support, and we were expecting the enemy to attack.

We were on extremely high alert, and the days kept dragging on, two, three, four, five.... The guys all thought each new day would be the one when we received orders to return to base.

Each day the word would spread: "We're going back to base today. Today, we're definitely going back."

By Day Five, all of the chow was gone.

By the night of our sixth day on the mountain, I had one can of food left, a little tin of ham the size of the tuna cans that you see in grocery stores.

I'd eaten all of my other rations by Day Four and toughed it out with everyone else, but by Day Six, I was shaking from the hunger.

That can was my emergency supply, and it was the only food in camp. Ten of us were sitting around when I told the guys I had it and pulled it out.

"Oh my God, food! Oh my God! Oh my God! Thank you! Thank you!"

The can held three pieces of ham, each about a quarter-inch thick, and we all took out our knives and cut them into even slices, like little slivers of pie. We each took our portion and ate it like it was the best food in the world. We were starved, and going to bed with a little food in our stomachs carried us through.

We finally received orders to come down on Day Seven, and the descent was a lot easier than going up. The trail became smoother, more gravelly, as men kept moving down, and at one point, this pudgy guy about four Marines up the hill behind me lost his footing.

He was loaded down like a mule, carrying his M16 and probably eighty pounds more of war gear, and he gained momentum the more he slid. I just stepped aside as he went past.

"Fuck him," I thought. "He could've wiped me out, too."

We had that little bit of food in our stomachs and we were finally coming down the mountain. We were giddy, and we all laughed at the sliding fool.

I remember being so thankful for my Jewish upbringing.

20

R&R Adventures

If we could make it through five or six months in a combat zone, we were entitled to a break. The Marine Corps gave five days of R&R, and we could choose between Singapore, Hong Kong and Thailand. Married officers could fly to Hawaii and meet their wives.

I chose Hong Kong. Wherever we were in Vietnam, the Corps flew us to Da Nang before R&R and assigned us to a captain. Mine was responsible for 150 Marines ready to relax, and at the Hong Kong airport, he gathered us around.

"OK, we use the buddy system on R&R. I'm going to pair each one of you guys up, and each one is responsible for each other. We're all due back here in five days at exactly this time, 1300 hours. If you're not here, you're AWOL."

AWOL means absent without leave, and it's about equal to desertion. The Corps doesn't screw around with something like that.

By coincidence, I got partnered up with one of the guys from my boot camp platoon. We headed out to one of the hotels in Hong Kong that catered to American servicemen. Our room was nice enough, just like a regular hotel room in New York City, but that wasn't a concern of mine.

"To hell with the room. Let's look for some girls!"

While the war was transforming us into men, we still were boys at heart. The military trained us to be killers, but looking for girls came naturally. Free time was rare, and we never knew which day could be our last, so instinct and desire took over whenever we were left to our own devices.

It has been a fact of war for as long as men have fought. It also is a fact that a Marine looking for girls might find trouble just as easily, no matter on which continent he might stand.

––––––

After my tour of Vietnam, I was sent on a Sixth Fleet "Med cruise," which is what we called operations based from Navy ships in the Mediterranean Sea. Shore leave always meant trips to the brothels.

The whorehouses in France looked a lot like Manhattan brownstones, five floors tall and very nice. I was in Marseilles, Cannes, Nice, and I always seemed to gravitate to the brothels there.

All that I could think was, "God, these girls are gorgeous."

I was always very respectful, and afterward I took them out to cafes and for walks and enjoyed the feel of a pretty girl on my arm.

The other guys would be jealous, "Who the fuck are you, walking around with a gorgeous girl?"

All that I could ever think to say was, "I want to marry her," and the girls would get a big laugh out of that. I actually meant it, too.

At one point during our Med cruise we were on the island of Corfu, and our job for a month and a half was to participate in war games with the armies from European countries that were our allies in World War II. The Marine Corps still had us training together. The operation was really huge, about five hundred Marines and the same number of troops from the European countries.

I had twelve guys under my command, and we trained all day, but the nights were a breeze compared with Vietnam. Nobody was going to kill us. We had our own little area out in the middle of all this farmland and could pitch two-man pup tents and build little fires.

Greek villagers leading donkeys and mules would come around at night peddling ouzo to the Marines for about fifty cents a bottle.

Ouzo tastes like licorice and is as thick as syrup. It is Greece's answer to absinthe, and I knew from the start that I didn't like it. It's like getting drunk on wine. Makes me feel like crap the next day.

After a little while, the ouzo peddlers expanded their product offering. "Girls! You want girls? Girls!"

Girls caught my attention!

When I'd gotten used to the routine, I started to get ideas, and one night I made a deal with one of the village men.

"Tomorrow night I bring girls," he said.

The next night, the guy showed up in a huge, battered truck.

"I must take you where girls are."

That wasn't the deal I thought I had struck. There was a huge language barrier, but jerky me, with my horns straight up in the air, I said, "Yeah, OK, fine, fine, fine."

So I asked my squad, "Who wants to get laid?"

Every hand shot up, the whole squad. That would be dereliction of duty for everyone to leave. I decided to make one guy stay and cover our area, in case some flunky or sergeant came along.

I figured I'd still be in trouble, but it might not be as serious as dereliction of duty. With girls on my mind, I wasn't thinking straight.

So my men and I got on the beat-up truck and headed out into the dark, bouncing around blind in the back. I had no idea where we were, and I was in charge. I started to panic after a few minutes.

"I can't speak the language. What if the truck breaks down? Where are we? What do I do?"

It was enough to lose a stripe, and I am a good Marine.

I was about ready to demand that the driver turn the truck around and take us back when this hillbilly-looking ghost town village popped up.

One building looked like a huge World War II era Quonset hut, and all of the lights were on. The driver pulled up beside it, and we all took that as our signal to jump out and go in.

It was like a gymnasium inside, and one hundred or two hundred Marines were already there. Other Marines! I was so relieved. I thought I was unique, being cool, being the first one to do this. But I wasn't the only horny squad leader in Greece.

Girls were on eight to ten mattresses with their legs up in the air, and Marines were waiting on line in front of each girl.

It was like chow line in a mess hall. Guys were talking, telling jokes, laughing, whatever. Then the line would move. The next Marine would mount, enjoy a few moments of intimacy, and then let the next Marine on line take a turn.

Hump, hump, hump. Next! Hump, hump, hump. Next! Just like that. We had to give like $2 or $4 to the guy who drove us, and he probably split it with the girls.

We had to be back at our assigned position at 0500, and we didn't get there until about thirty minutes before. None of us slept a wink. At twenty years old, we had the stamina to march the whole day without sleep.

I was proud of myself. I pulled it off, never got in trouble, except… When we were sent back to the ship, we infested the holds with crabs. The whole ship came down with crabs—crabs all over everything.

I had crabs so bad that it took me more than a year to get rid of them. Even after I was discharged from the Marines, I still had crabs, Greek crabs.

———

My first R&R break from Vietnam left lingering reminders of different sorts.

After six months of getting shot at in a jungle, Hong Kong was a shock, but a cool shock. I really appreciated civilization. I wasn't in America, but it was great: stores, sidewalks, electricity, lights, hot food, bars—and girls.

I took about $300. We usually couldn't spend money in Vietnam. We got paid, but we had nowhere to spend the money, so we saved up for R&R and spent our pay on things that really didn't make a whole lot of sense.

Hong Kong is known for having good tailors, so my partner and I ended up getting fitted for clothes, and this tailor set me up with a suit, which would have done me no good in Vietnam, so I mailed it back to my parents.

The package probably stayed in the mail for a month. When it finally reached my parents and they opened it, it stunk like formaldehyde.

My mother couldn't take the smell, so she took it to the cleaner. When he brought it back, the suit stood on its own! I swear! It was like cardboard. The cleaner came and said, "Mrs. Fixler, you're not going to believe this, but your son's suit is cardboard."

That's how phony it was. We didn't know! We were just teenagers fresh from a war zone. What the hell did we know?

On our second day in Hong Kong, my R&R buddy and I decided to call home, and I told my parents that I'd sent the suit. My Marine partner was from a Navy family, and when he called his home, his father refused to talk to him.

His brother told him, "Dad's not going to talk to you. He's pissed off that you joined the Marines and you didn't join the Navy."

We had whiskey in our hotel room, of course, and his father's rejection upset him. He started guzzling whiskey and I wasn't really paying attention. I went about my business and didn't realize that he was getting bent out of shape because his father wouldn't talk to him.

I found out when he started punching all the glass in our room: the window, the lamps, and the mirrors. Boom! Boom! He totally lost control! Boom! Boom! Boom! It was almost as if a bull came into our room and destroyed the place.

Glass was everywhere, and so was his blood. I had to wrap towels around him and take him to the emergency center so that they could take the spikes of glass from his hand. He was insane.

We probably spent half a day in the emergency room. What the Hong Kong doctors did was so crude; it looked like he was wearing white boxing gloves made of gauze. They just kept wrapping bandages around his hands until they were useless mitts. We were Americans, and they probably couldn't have cared less. Not only were we Americans, we were moron Americans, so they just threw on a bunch of gauze bandages.

He was in pain and probably still had glass in him. I'm sure the glass infected him after three or four days, and his R&R was ruined. They gave him painkillers and he lay in bed for the next three days while I ran out and got laid.

On the day we had to meet back with the other Marines, the captain flipped out when he saw the guy's hands wrapped like two big boxing gloves.

"What the fuck happened to you?! What the fuck did you guys do?!"

I'm sure they had to put him in a hospital when we got back to Vietnam. Strange, but I was anxious to get back, very psyched.

Returning to Vietnam meant going from the relative comfort of Hong Kong back to having our necks on the line 24/7. The first time I had set foot in Vietnam had been after Camp Pendleton. We were bombarded with training, and then all of a sudden we were in Vietnam going on combat patrols and ambushes every day.

After I had been in the jungle and then received a five-day reminder of what civilian life was like, it was a little tough going back, but that didn't last.

There is a phenomenon that other people can verify: When you have bonded with a group of men, lived and fought with them, saved each other's lives, you worry about them.

I was thinking, "Brother, I just hope nothing major happened. I hope there were no firefights. I hope nobody got killed."

The last thing I wanted to hear was, "We lost twelve guys, four dead, eight wounded bad. We got overrun!"

I would have felt guilty if something had happened and I hadn't been there.

"Why did I have to pick this weekend? Why did I have to go?"

I would have been mad at myself, really mad.

Fortunately, that never happened during the times that I went on R&R. Oh, I missed out on being soaking wet and humping in the rain for five days during monsoon season, running out of water, running out of food, but I didn't mind avoiding those hardships.

But if something had gone down and they had needed me and something had happened to them, I would've been torn apart emotionally. We all felt that way.

I try to look tough at the Marine base in Phu Bai at the beginning of my tour in Vietnam.

I practice firing my M16 somewhere in Vietnam.

I stand in the middle of fellow Marines holding one of the unusually large care packages that my family would send me in Vietnam. After I fell from a helicopter onto a pile of mailbags and escaped injury, a fellow Marine, Matt Walsh, joked, "You probably survived because you landed on your own mailbags."

Looking tanned and tough, I prepare to go on combat patrol from the base at Phu Bai.

I bonded in Vietnam with "Skinny," who was one of my first combat mentors and helped teach me how to fight and survive. "Skinny" even visited my parents in New York after his tour in Vietnam, just to tell them that I was going to be OK.

One of my mentors, "Skinny," right, and two other
Marines pose for a picture in my family's Long Island
home while using one of their few precious days on leave
to visit my parents and tell them that I was doing well and
would make it home just fine.

A laughing Vietnamese child, bottom left, sits on my knee near
the "doomed bridge."

I'm in the middle wearing combat boots and civilian clothes that I must have borrowed from one of the guys. We had just come out of Jewish services during my in-country R&R. They were among the few other Jews that I met on the Da Nang combat base.

I strike a bad-ass pose before going on patrol from the Phu Bai combat base.

I aim my M16 at someone or something. I don't remember the moment, but it looks intense.

I had to carry my 3.5-inch rocket launcher, aka bazooka, on company-sized operations, but it was useless on combat patrols.

My R&R buddy and I pose with our bellhop in Hong Kong in our new "cardboard" suits.

I write a letter to home early in my tour of Vietnam.

I wrote the note of reassurance to my parents on the back of this photograph and didn't see it again until 2010.

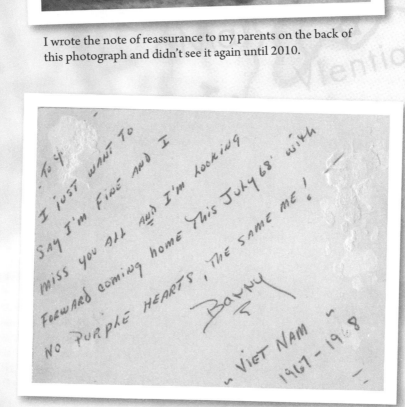

To ye
I just want to say I'm fine and I miss you all and I'm looking forward coming home this July 68' with NO PURPLE HEARTS, The same me!

Barry

Viet Nam 1967 - 1968

I wrote this note to reassure my family. My choice of words, "the same me!" tells me that I knew my personality would not be adversely affected by the extreme violence of combat.

At far left is Mike Lucas next to "Skinny," then me, on November 16, 1967, at the base at Phu Bai.

Mike Lucas, left, and Anthony Wood pose for a picture at Phu Bai. They'd become fast friends, but Wood was destined to die heroically while defending hill 861-A at Khe Sanh.

KHE SANH

21

Making Men and Heroes

"In reaffirming the greatness of our nation, we understand that greatness is never a given. It must be earned. Our journey has never been one of shortcuts or settling for less. It has not been the path for the faint-hearted—for those who prefer leisure over work, or seek only the pleasures of riches and fame. Rather, it has been the risk-takers, the doers, the makers of things—some celebrated but more often men and women, obscure in their labor, who have carried us up the long, rugged path towards prosperity and freedom. For us, they packed up their few worldly possessions and traveled across oceans in search of a new life. For us, they toiled in sweatshops and settled the West; endured the lash of the whip and plowed the hard earth. For us, they fought and died, in places like Concord and Gettysburg, Normandy and Khe Sanh."

—President Barack Obama
Jan. 20, 2009, inaugural address on the National Mall,
Washington, D.C.

———

We either became men or we became statistics at the Siege of Khe Sanh. Those who became statistics were the real men. They were the heroes. Khe Sanh may not have altered the outcome of the war, but it added to the mystique of the Marine Corps because despite overwhelming odds, we refused to lose.

Khe Sanh was a village in the Quang Tri Province of South Vietnam, just below the 17th Parallel and the Demilitarized Zone, and the site of the Marines' Khe Sanh Combat Base and airstrip.

The seventy-seven-day siege that the North Vietnamese launched on January 21, 1968, was the longest and deadliest battle of the Vietnam War, and was so important in the mind of President Lyndon B. Johnson that he had a sand model of the battlefield built in the White House situation room and demanded daily updates from his Joint Chiefs of Staff. LBJ feared that the battle would become his Dien Bien Phu, the battle the North Vietnamese won to effectively end French colonialism in Vietnam in 1954.

Nobody agrees on the exact number of casualties on either side. No one even knows. Many men died weeks, months, and even years after the official siege ended, in cold, faraway hospital beds, and more still returned to their homes but left limbs or parts of their souls to wither in the blood-soaked dirt of those jungle hills.

Regardless of whose numbers are used, Marines took the heaviest casualties of all the U.S. military branches that served at Khe Sanh. In his book *Battalion of Kings*, Chaplain Ray William Stubbe said that 456 Marines died at Khe Sanh from January 20, 1968 (just before the official start of the siege) to April 16, 1968 (a week after), along with 83 Army troops, 23 from the Navy and 7 from the Air Force.

Marines easily caught the worst hell, accounting for almost three-quarters of the U.S. deaths, but inflicted far more on the North Vietnamese. Some estimates put their number of deaths at as many as 20,000 men. They hit us with everything they could, firing artillery from fixed positions in Laos and rockets and mortars from right under our noses, and we held our ground.

The enemy moved so close to our lines that the Air Force, confident in the ability and precision of its B-52s and their crews, changed its tactics and began dropping bombs nearly on top of us, with devastating consequences for the North Vietnamese.

The bombing never stopped, and one of my vivid memories is the near constant rain of dirt and rocks on our heads from the explosions of NVA artillery and our own "friendly" bombs.

Even as we were defeating the North Vietnamese, the Tet Offensive was changing the nature of the conflict. But ours was a defined objective and a clear victory. I became a man at Khe Sanh, a man with a huge and lifelong extended family. In doing so, I saw many Marines killed and many more seriously wounded.

22

A Climb Into Hell

The top of what became known as Hill 861-A was just virgin land covered with elephant grass and bamboo when I first saw it. My company, Echo 2/26, had to claw through the dense vegetation and up the steep slopes of what would become a bomb-scarred hilltop with trenches reminiscent of World War I battles. In fact, over the next seventy-seven days Khe Sanh would earn the dubious record of receiving the heaviest bombardment of a small area in the history of warfare.

———

All we knew in mid-January of 1968 was that we were leaving Phu Bai for a place called Khe Sanh and were loaded down with war gear, all that we could carry. I only knew of it as a company operation, and how it affected me, Lance Corporal Barry Fixler. I was unaware that we were part of a huge, regiment-size operation. None of us had a clue.

They put our whole company in a huge C-130 transport plane, and it seemed that this operation might be a little bigger than most. But that was all. We knew we were going to an area closer than Phu Bai to the DMZ, so it probably would be worse than Phu Bai had been, but I was a seasoned Marine with six months of combat, so I was unworried, confident.

The DMZ—Demilitarized Zone—was anything but. It was a narrow band of territory at the 17th Parallel through part of which the Ben Hai River ran. It marked the line of partition of Vietnam into North and South Vietnam in accordance with the Geneva Accords signed between Vietnam and France in 1954.

The DMZ was intended to exist as a zone free from any military presence by either North or South for a limited period until national unification elections took place. But history didn't follow the script written by the diplomats. The zone and the areas around it saw some of the greatest destruction and carnage of the war.

After we landed at the Khe Sanh combat base and organized, we humped outside the lines and into the fields. We dug in on a small hill the first couple of nights. There was no outpost. We were the only Marines there, and we still did not know what our objective was or what actually was happening.

We all had an eerie, uneasy feeling, though. Whatever we were doing, it wasn't routine. We knew that we were in a bad spot; we just didn't know how bad.

We finally ended up at the base of a steep hill, a mountain almost, about 2,500 feet high. There was only one overgrown trail, so the 150 or so of us started up it in a single column. The terrain was horrible and took hours to climb.

I carried a rocket launcher that looked like a huge bazooka, my M16 rifle and ammunition, all of my grenades, my gas mask and a minimum of two rockets.

That's a heavy load, and we still had to be alert for an ambush at any second.

The hill was very steep and the trail was overgrown, but carrying everything required both of my hands, so I couldn't use them to help myself up. It was a real struggle, and the heat was oppressive.

We were given no breaks to rest. We were screwed—very vulnerable and spread too thin. I still think we were lucky that we reached the top without being slaughtered. The NVA were probably saying, "What the fuck?!" They must have been able to see us.

We fought the tangled growth and slipped on the sandy ground, and at one point, I lost my temper and began beating on my rocket launcher with my hands.

"Fuck! Fuck! Fuck! Fuck! I can't believe this! This is fucking tough!"

We were the first Marines to reach the top of 861-A, and not a soul was there, just wild grass, bamboo, and other vegetation all over the place. We had obscured lines of sight, which would make it difficult to find targets when we had to shoot back at whoever would inevitably start shooting at us. The enemy could have sneaked up to within ten feet of us and we wouldn't have been able to see him. It was horrible.

So the first thing we did was start digging.

Darkness was falling on us fast, and we were totally out of water. The only moisture that we could find was on bamboo shoots that were covered with mites. I remember snapping the bamboo rods and putting our tongues to them to catch the drops of water as they trickled out.

It was that way for the next two or three days as we continued to entrench ourselves and clear our lines of fire. Someone erected an American flag. We didn't get the barbed wire and concertina razor wire emplaced around our position for about a week, so it was a good thing that the NVA didn't zero in on us quickly. It would've been really nasty if they had.

Hill 861 already was getting pounded and had been overrun once, and within three days or so we started catching mortars and rockets on 861-A. Each day grew more intense, and we got the feel-

ing that we might be there for awhile, but we had no way of knowing that it would turn into seventy-seven days of hell.

The NVA became increasingly better at aiming their mortars,
rockets, and artillery. They would rain mortars up and down the
lines. Ba-boom! Ba-boom! Ba-boom! We even were hit with our
own artillery a few times. Things like that just happened, and we
felt helpless against it.

23

Learning to Survive

The first week of February 1968, the NVA really turned it on. They shelled us hard, worse than usual. The rockets and mortars were almost constant.

On February 4, a chopper came in to evacuate the wounded and bring in replacements and supplies. The new guys ran off the chopper, and I ran on to offload supplies.

Heavy rockets and mortars showered the landing zone, and as the chopper lifted off, I jumped into a trench and ended up next to one of the new guys. He had been in Vietnam for a day or two, and on the hill for all of one minute. He was clearly shaken by the intensity of the situation.

"How long you been in country?" he asked.

"Six months," I told him

"How could you live that long? How's that possible?"

I remember the conversation because the new Marine's name reminded me of the actor Humphrey Bogart. He was killed the next day.

Too many Marines were killed on Hill 861-A on February 5, 1968, when we were totally overrun.

The North Vietnamese swarmed in from all directions. They were all over the hill. Three or four Marines were right there when the first NVA popped up, and they just got overrun. The shooting was intense, and waves of enemy soldiers just kept coming, coming, coming, coming, coming, coming, coming.

Everything went down at once: artillery, rockets, mortars, small arms, bayonets, even tear gas. It took us all night to kill all the North Vietnamese in our lines.

I heard more of the fighting on February 5 than I saw. I spent the night back-to-back with another Marine holding our position in the trenches. The enemy was so close, swarming over and through our trenches that there was a serious risk of shooting one of our own guys.

So another Marine and I instinctively ended up with our backs to each other, holding our position in the trench line. It was total chaos, pitch black, and the constant explosions from rockets, artillery, and grenades created a strobe-light effect.

And we used gas grenades on the NVA. Tear gas is heavier than air and it blew back on us and filled our trenches. So we also had to wear our gas masks that night, which limited our vision even more. Our ears rang from the constant explosions, and each flash of light from the blasts briefly illuminated a portrait of death through the gas mask goggles.

It was like being blindfolded and spun around fifty times. Then they take off the blindfold, flip the lights on and off, blast your ears with noise loud enough to make your nose bleed, and you have to try to identify and shoot the enemy… all night long.

You don't have time in a situation like that to note individual acts of heroism, but as I found out later, my mentor, Tom Eichler, was a hero that night.

Hill 861-A could well have fallen if Tom hadn't done the things that he did, and that would have changed the entire course of the war. His actions were emblematic of what made Khe Sanh a part of Marine Corps lore: perseverance against overwhelming odds.

Three of our men manning a machine gun were injured when the NVA overran their position in the initial assault. Three times Tom dodged enemy fire to carry each of the men to safety.

He killed three NVA in hand-to-hand combat, stopping them from firing a rocket into a trench filled with Marines. When the enemy managed to establish a machine gun position inside our perimeter, Tom wiped it out with grenades, and he sprayed cover fire that allowed our own machine gunners to move into a position to defend us.

He stood above the trenches to throw grenades down on the advancing enemy, and the entire time he made sure that we were kept supplied with ammunition. Tom was seriously injured early in the assault but his injuries never slowed him.

When dawn came, we counted 109 North Vietnamese bodies sliced and diced all over the hill. I remember thinking, "What? Another one? Fuck! Another one. Another one."

I was impressed because I expected to see about half that number.

Even spread over maybe two acres, 109 was a lot of bodies. We had seven Marines killed, and far too many wounded.

I remember taking Marines out of the trenches and carrying them in ponchos to our landing zone to be evacuated to a field hospital.

I don't know the exact numbers, but I remember personally seeing at least thirty seriously wounded Marines: guys missing limbs, or so damaged that they probably died within a few days. At best, they lived but never fought again.

We waded through the trenches and gathered the wounded and dead. And after a corpsman had stabilized a wounded Marine, we wrapped him in a poncho and carried him to a staging area near the LZ.

One of the guys I helped suffered multiple severe injuries, and

I talked to him to try to keep him from going into shock. He asked me to find his hand.

"I need my hand. Can you look for my hand?"

I asked where his fighting hole was and told him I'd look for it. I meant it, too. But when I got to his area and started looking around, reality set in. Debris and body parts were everywhere.

"Barry, it's hopeless," I thought. "Even if you find a whole hand, there's no way to know if it's his."

One of the guys in my squad, Jim Kaylor, saw a severed leg fall out of a poncho as two Marines carried a wounded Marine to the LZ. Jim picked up the leg and handed it back to the wounded Marine boot-end first; It's inconsiderate to hand a wounded Marine the bloody end of his leg.

It was brutal. We just kept lining them up, and helicopters came and choppered them away. The dead NVA outnumbered our casualties about ten to one.

We needed immediate reinforcements, and when they came from other units, they all wore looks in their eyes that said, "Oh my God, I'm fucked! I am fucked!"

We didn't put their minds at ease.

"They're definitely gonna attack us again tonight," I told the green Marines. "Be ready because they're coming back. Those motherfuckers are coming back tonight!"

The new guys all were wide-eyed and solemn, and you could tell that they were thinking, "Ah shit, I'm gonna die tonight! Fuck! I'm gonna die tonight!"

Those of us who had been on the hill since the beginning didn't think that way. By that time, those of us who were still alive *were* tough Marines.

I looked at myself sometimes and couldn't see the green Marine who had landed in the country only six months earlier. I was just fucking hell-bent to kill the enemy, just fucking kill 'em, kick their motherfucking asses.

It was more like, "C'mon, you gave us your best shot yesterday, and now give us your best shot today!"

"We kicked your asses last night and we're gonna fuck you up again tonight!"

In no way could I show fear to the new guys. I had to raise my confidence to a new level.

Those guys picked up on that real fast, and pretty soon, the ones who survived, they talked the same shit. They needed to see the example to have that confidence, and then they fed off of it.

When they overran us so early into everything, we didn't expect it. But thereafter, it was, "Motherfucker! Bring it!"

I don't know what the proper term is. It rattled us but it didn't scare us. It was more like, "Yeah, come on, let's get it on! Here, you want to fuck with us?! Let's try this again! Come on!"

And they did. The NVA continued to bring it. They never overran our position again, but they laid siege to us for another two months, even longer, throwing everything they could at us: artillery, rockets, mortars, and grenades.

———

Long after the siege, when my ears had quit ringing, I still thought sometimes that I could smell the gas.

Anyone who ever has been gassed will tell you that things can't get much more fucked up. Unless you've experienced it and found the discipline within yourself to apply your training and overcome it, you can't control yourself. You can have the best rifle in the world, but it's worthless against gas.

The night the NVA overran us, I was moving from off watch to on when the skies lit up and we scrambled to organize and fight back, and then I smelled the gas. The odor is distinct and unforgettable. I didn't know that we were using the gas. I assumed it was the NVA gassing us, or that a Marine had been blown up and his gas grenades exploded with him.

I was seasoned then and thought I was cool, and I'd let my hair grow nice and long. I didn't panic, but as I held my breath and put on my gas mask as I had learned in boot camp, the band of it tangled in my hair, and the only thing that I could do was start yanking my hair out by the roots. It was like pulling clumps of grass out of an overgrown lawn.

My head had been shaved during boot camp, the last time that I had do the gas mask procedure, but doing it with long hair while under enemy fire was a whole different matter. I cleared the tangled spot, fit the mask on and blew to clear the gas from inside and I was ready to fight, but I was pissed at myself for not getting a haircut.

Fighting a real enemy while wearing a gas mask is more than difficult. You're looking through goggles, and it doesn't help when one of the first things that you can see is that a lot of your guys are dead or seriously wounded. We lost a lot of Marines that day. They can't simulate that experience in boot camp.

———

It's not that the drill instructors at boot camp didn't try.

At one point during recruit training at Parris Island, South Carolina, the drill instructors had a platoon of eighty or ninety of us seated on bleachers outside.

We were seated at attention, our backs straight, our faces expressionless and all eyes and ears trained on the drill instructor standing in front of us. He held a live rabbit, a nice, little, white bunny rabbit that he petted as he talked. I forget his topic because, as it turned out, that wasn't the day's lesson.

He kept talking and petting the rabbit for several minutes, until it became almost invisible to us. We listened intently to him and paid little if any attention to the rabbit. Then, in a flash and for no apparent reason, the drill instructor seized the rabbit tight and snapped its neck, just snapped it!

Blood gushed from the rabbit's mouth, and some poor recruit reacted.

"Aaaghhhhhh!"

We all were caught off guard, but the one guy showed it more than the rest of us, and the drill instructor hurled the bleeding bunny into his chest, and it fell into his lap. Its guts oozed from its throat.

The recruit had no choice but to sit there covered in the rabbit's blood and guts as it lay dead in his lap. He couldn't move.

"Holy shit!" I thought, but the lesson was pretty clear: Always be ready for the unexpected, and show no fear or any other emotions.

Learning to use gas masks was much the same.

Before we ever went in the gas chamber, they taught us how to put on a gas mask while we were seated as a group on bleachers outdoors. Several hundred of us recruits were out there, and a drill instructor demonstrated the proper technique.

If you already have been exposed to gas and you just put on the mask tight and breathe, you're going to suck up that gas. So there's a way—after you get it on tight with the rubber straps while holding your breath—that you hold the edges and blow out, and that expels whatever gas already was inside the mask, and then you can breathe.

That's the procedure, and it's hard to do at first. You can't see, and you have to hold your breath because if you inhale too much gas, you're done for. You'll shit, you'll piss, and all sorts of crap will come out of your nostrils while you're gasping for air. You're blinded. You want to touch your skin because it's being affected, but if you do, you will only irritate it more. It's hypersensitive and painful to the lightest touch.

You have no control of your body, and you're in no shape to fight. All you can think to do is run away, screaming like a lunatic.

I didn't really understand all of that while sitting in a group in the bleachers, practicing putting on the masks, holding my breath for a minute or more, blowing to expel the imaginary gas, doing all of that.

It seemed easy. It took some time until everyone could get the technique down to where we all could do it in less than a minute, but still, we were outside in nice fresh air, and it was easy.

Then, the drill instructor yelled, "Any recruit that needs to practice more, let me hear it! Does every recruit know how to do this within one minute?"

"Yes, sir!" we answered in unison.

"Are you ready to go to the gas chamber?"

"Yes, sir!"

Half of us weren't—hell, hardly any of us were—but nobody wanted to be the guy to admit that. You never want to be singled out in Marine Corps recruit training.

What we didn't know was that two other drill instructors were sneaking beneath the bleachers while we sat above them lying.

"Yes, sir! We know! Yes, sir! We know! Yes, sir! We can do it!"

But we all were scared shitless of the chamber because once you're in there, you're fucked. You'd better know what you were doing.

The drill instructor in front of us gave a signal and the two drill instructors that we didn't know about under the bleachers set off gas grenades, and all hell broke loose.

Half of the recruits, including me, tried to run. It was a cluster fuck. We were blind, stumbling and bumping into each other and pissing ourselves, shitting ourselves, nasty chunks and goo flying from our nostrils.

We couldn't function.

I saw everyone else gasping, gagging and flailing, and then I realized, "Holy shit, I'm doing the same fucking thing!"

But that was a lesson that we all had to learn. It took several minutes for things to calm down, and about half of the guys did well. I was in the half that didn't, but at least I wasn't singled out.

"Now fucking pay attention!" the drill instructor barked. "Because this shit is not gonna happen when you get in the fucking gas chamber!"

" Yes sir!" we all answered.

The gas chamber didn't come until near the end of boot camp, and all recruits feared it. The feeling is like being put in a coffin and having the lid shut over you and sealed.

But by the time we actually went into the gas chamber, almost all of us were ready. I did just fine. Out of the thirty or so recruits that went in together, only one guy would freak out and turn into a lunatic, and the drill instructors just let him go wild.

The guy would be trying to escape the gas chamber through the steel hatch, and the harder he tried, the worse it got for him. We didn't feel sorry for those guys. You had to fucking learn. I was glad that it wasn't me.

24

Somebody is Going to Die

Second lieutenants and squad leaders passed through a revolving door of death at Khe Sanh, which was where I was promoted to a squad leader. It wasn't long before I began asking myself how long I could last.

New second lieutenants were always coming in. More men in that rank were probably killed, by percentage, than those in any other rank, and squad leaders couldn't have been far behind.

Second lieutenants had no credibility; that was something that had to be earned. Second lieutenant was the lowest rank for an officer. They had just finished training in the States. What war did they have in the States? No war.

On top of that, second lieutenants came into units full of seasoned Marines who had been in combat for a year or more. The officers probably trained as hard or harder than the enlisted men, though. First they had to go through four years of college, and then through officer's candidate school and training, but they had no combat experience.

Second lieutenants had to be in the worst spot at all times because they were leaders. They had to be where the bad stuff was happening at every moment, and so they were vulnerable. The position of squad leader among the enlisted men was based on who had been in the squad longest when rotations came, and on who still was alive and able to fight.

Becoming a squad leader meant the world to me, but I suddenly had responsibility for anywhere from seven to twelve guys.

Every morning, squad leaders from my platoon had to report to the command post (CP). The order would get passed down the trench line, "Squad leaders up!"

That meant that I had to run as low as possible through trenches to get to the CP, where Captain Earle Breeding waited. I usually was ducking from mortars and rockets.

The CP was a little sandbag hut in which six to ten guys could fit, but we had to sit. There was no room to stand because a taller structure would have been a big target.

Captain Breeding barked out orders, telling us our jobs for the day, what our plan was.

"OK, first platoon, you're doing good. Mortars. Where's mortars? Where's machine guns?"

Maybe Captain Breeding would want an extra listening post, an LP. That was the worst of the worst. They sent two men out at night past the edge of our perimeter, the other side of the razor wire, to listen for the enemy and notify us if they heard them. It was like throwing them to the dogs. They were cannon fodder.

Or he could order a squad to go out and clean up C-ration cans that were carelessly thrown out past the perimeter.

"First platoon? Send a squad out to police the area south of your line. We have animals out there scavenging your C-rats and we're gonna get complacent. Next time the enemy probes the line, we'll think its rats!"

Maybe he would order us to repair the concertina wire. A working party. "Third platoon, send a working party out there and throw more wire."

We were always busy. There was always something to do. We never sat around. We survived by staying busy, and if we weren't assigned to a working party, we had to dig deeper and pile sandbags higher.

Captain Breeding gave us these orders every morning, and as I got used to being a squad leader, I began to notice, "Whoa, another new face! Oh my God, another new face!"

I saw the same faces for a few days, and then one would be gone and replaced by someone new. Sometimes guys just got rotated back to the States, but most of the time they were wounded or killed. I would think, "Oh my God, another new face! Oh no! That guy got fucked up! That guy replaced Wilson. Wilson got fucked up."

I'd wonder, "Whoa, who's going to replace me when I get it?"

Years later I saw the movie *Spartacus* with Kirk Douglas, and for some reason one of the scenes reminded me of our morning meetings with Captain Breeding.

Before they called Spartacus and his opponent into the ring in which one of them would die, the two warriors sat in a little room and stared at each other, knowing that one of them was doomed.

That's the exact feeling I had when I sat in the squad leaders' meeting. It was just like the two gladiators in *Spartacus*. I would look at the faces and know someone was going to die. It's just a very heavy feeling. No one wanted anybody to die, but that was the situation. Somebody was going to die.

I would look at their faces and think, "Who's the next one to die? Who is the next one to die? Am I next?"

I never thought, though, that it might be from a bullet from one of our guys. That nearly happened.

One of our jobs at Khe Sanh was to patrol the valley between Hills 861 and 861-A. The valley was total death. It was from there that the NVA launched mortars at us. They were down there in their territory and we were up on the hills, and they did everything they could to knock us off. The valley was nothing but jungle, the worst of the worst. We would walk down into it, and about thirty or forty feet outside of our perimeter, we would just disappear into the dense vegetation.

Each mission lasted a few hours. We would hump down one hill, through the valley, and up the other hill. Sometimes we stayed there overnight and came back the next day, but other times we made the trip in one day.

These patrols were always during the day. Night patrols would have been suicide missions. As it was, walking out there was just the same as saying to the enemy, "Please shoot at me."

Fortunately, I never had to walk point. That was the most dangerous patrol job, for obvious reasons. I was in weapons platoon and it was not our job to walk point. Walking point took elephant balls.

On one patrol between the hills, I was about three or four guys behind the Marine on point. There were probably eight of us, and we walked slowly, serious as can be. We just knew that the enemy would hit us. We were about halfway between the hills when I heard a loud BOOM and felt a burst of air between my boots.

My brain told me that I'd just stepped on a Bouncing Betty. They could shred you. I saw guys get hit by Bouncing Bettys, and it always was ugly. I had seen enough combat by that time to know that the odds of losing my legs were far greater than they were of getting killed. Making it out of Vietnam without losing at least one leg seemed almost impossible.

"Don't look now, Barry," I thought. "Wait for the pain."

The other Marines took cover as soon as they heard the explosion. I froze and waited for the pain to come up to my head and to go back down. I didn't want to look at my legs. I had heard the explosion and felt the pressure and dirt flying, and I just waited for the pain. ...

Nothing. ...

After a few seconds, I looked down and saw feet, normal feet. My feet.

My brain already had started coping with losing my legs.

"It caught up to you, Barry. You're going to lose your legs, just like everybody else. We all lose our legs."

But I looked down and everything was normal, and then I heard a Marine behind me.

"Fuck, it was me!"

Everyone was still on the ground. He and I were the only ones still standing, and I turned to him.

"What do you mean it was you?!"

"I wasn't sure if my safety was on or off so I pulled the trigger; I really thought that my safety was on. It was stupid."

His rifle was pointed exactly between my boots when he pulled the trigger. I was extremely lucky. We had close calls every day, but that one stands out because it was unusual to get shot, or nearly shot, by another Marine.

We regrouped and got up the other hill, and then we took the time to say a few "What the fucks!" But we didn't dwell on what had gone down. Anything can happen at war.

25

Magnet Mike Lucas

The siege of Khe Sanh was living hell only if you were lucky enough to stay alive, hunkered down in trenches under constant artillery, mortar and rocket fire. It was as crude as things get, but we were Marines: Our morale was up.

It got to a point when we were being mortared that we didn't ask, "Did anybody get hit?" It was, "Who got hit?"

We took casualties at all hours and from all directions. Sometimes the helicopters would drop in reinforcements, but they were never enough.

Strange, but a person gets used to being bombed every day. It's the truth. You really do. It's survival of the fittest. You could pitch a pup tent in the middle of one of New York City's busiest streets, and after a while, you learn how to survive there, given the opportunity.

We always were low on food, at best two meals a day instead of three, if you rated what they compressed into two little C-ration cans as a meal. The cans were tiny, maybe an inch tall and three inches in diameter. We had to ration our water, too.

What each of us got in our cans was luck of the draw. Each case of rations had twelve different types of meals, and someone would flip the box and we'd pick from the upside-down cans so that no guy could see what he was getting.

Lucky might mean beef chips. My favorite was compressed spaghetti in tomato sauce; it looked like dog food. When I knocked it out of the can, it would hold its shape just like dog food. I had to mash it up some to make it a little more edible.

Unlucky meant ham and motherfuckers. Ham and motherfuckers were lima beans and chips of ham. Lima beans! They were disgusting, so we called them ham and motherfuckers. Nobody wanted ham and motherfuckers, but out of a case of twelve meals, one guy in the squad had to get the ham and motherfuckers. Guys would get their cans, and soon enough we would hear, "Fuck! Ham and motherfuckers! Fuck, man, I got the ham and motherfuckers!"

We were always ready to exploit new guys who didn't know any better, to con them into a trade and stick them with the ham and motherfuckers.

"Hey, cool! I got the ham and motherfuckers! You wanna switch?"

———

One day in mid-February, during a rare break in the incoming, Mike Lucas called to me from two foxholes over. Mike was one of my best friends, and for whatever reasons he always thought that it was really funny that one of our Marines almost shot me in the legs.

"Hey Fix! Fix! Fix! Hey Fix, I got something cool!"

"What the hell could he have that's cool?" I thought. Nothing had changed for weeks. No mail, ham and motherfuckers, nothing had changed. "What could he have that's cool?"

"I have cupcakes!"

"How the fuck could you have cupcakes?" I asked him. We were under siege, living in trenches, men dying. How could he have cupcakes?

We would get these tins of compressed pound cake, and every

so often our C-rations included miniature Hershey bars. Mike got creative.

We always had C4, which is an explosive that's a little like Play-Doh. During the day, but never at night, we could use little pinches of it to heat our food. Without a detonator, it wouldn't explode, but it would burn. We would light the C4, place an empty can upside down over it, then put the can with our food in it on top of that. It was like a little burner, and it made the food a little easier to get down.

Mike must have formed the pound cake into three little cupcakes, and then melted his Hershey bars and dripped the chocolate over the pound cake. He presented it to me and another Marine, Lance Corporal James Anthony Wood, really nice on a piece of cardboard, like he was a chef or something.

Like a jerk, I didn't catch on right away. It didn't dawn on me that he could have just made the cupcakes.

"Where did you get those cupcakes?"

"Some helicopter guy just flew in them in for us."

It really didn't matter. Mike, James and I probably spent ten minutes just admiring those little cupcakes, and then we only ate them in nibbles, nice and slow—three tough Marines giggling like school kids and eating cute Khe Sanh cupcakes.

That was James Wood's last treat.

———

On February 25, 1968, the NVA had zeroed in on one area so well that it was almost certain death. Around sunset, one of the corporals found me.

"Fixler," he told me, "we lost three Marines; no one has their hole. Give up one of the men from your squad. Someone has to be in that hole."

The position was totally vacant. We had lost so many Marines in that foxhole that I just knew whoever I put in that hole was a dead man.

Mike Lucas and I met back in July 1967 in Phu Bai. We were both from New York, and we hit it off right away. We had similar personalities. We were buddies from then on and stayed on the same operations and in the same platoon.

Then James Anthony Wood was attached to our squad, and he and Mike Lucas became extremely close. They shared the same hole and always were hanging out and laughing. I was nineteen years old, and I got a little jealous: "Jesus Christ! I'm losing my best friend."

So when the corporal told me I had to give up a man to replace the ones who had been blown out of that doomed foxhole, I had to make a decision real quick. It was almost a certain death sentence.

I made a call—Wood—and he manned that hole. Knowing the kind of guy he was, Mike volunteered to go with him.

"We're going in together."

Wood was killed within hours of my decision. The foxhole took a direct hit from a mortar after dark.

"Minutes before, we were talking about home, watching through binoculars," Mike said years later, "and the mortars started coming in and he was completely disintegrated, no head at all."

Somehow Mike survived it, and when daylight came, he looked down at his flak jacket and saw part of James Wood's face. There were pieces of flesh, and the stubble from Wood's beard was impaled in the protective jacket, little hairs just standing erect.

It was a heavy blow to Mike and I could tell it shook him up. Mike was a tough Marine, a great Marine. That means James Anthony Wood was, too.

But as hard as it hit him, Mike had to shake it off, like we all had to. We were fighting a war, in a pitched battle, and we were taking losses daily. There was no time to reflect on our situation. We simply endured what had to be endured.

———

As much as I can still hear the echoes of the mortars and rockets in my head, I can also hear, "Corpsman up!"

That meant somebody was wounded and needed immediate medical attention.

Boom! Boom! Boom!

"Corpsman up! Corpsman up!"

Boom! Boom! Boom!

"Corpsman up! Corpsman up!"

It was that way all day, every day, and that made every day a tough one. The few men who rotated out were the lucky ones. Most only left if they were wounded or killed.

A Marine who received three Purple Hearts in one tour of duty would be rotated out and sent home.

Mike was a good Marine, a real good Marine, but he was a magnet for things like shrapnel. He was my friend, so I got him the hell out of Vietnam.

We were fighting on Hill 861-A when Mike caught shrapnel from a grenade, and it riddled his body. One piece lodged near his spinal cord, so close that doctors couldn't operate.

They evacuated him to a medical ship, the *USS Repose,* which was basically a floating Navy hospital, but two weeks hadn't passed before he was back on the hill.

"Holy shit!" I said. "What are you doing back here?"

He showed me all of his unhealed wounds from the grenade. It looked like he had been stabbed with a knife repeatedly. There were puncture wounds all over his neck, shoulder and chest, and each one was sutured.

"How the fuck can they send you back like this?"

"They sewed me up," he said. "I'm good to go! I got a Purple Heart!"

It wasn't a week later before Mike Lucas took it again, and he was back off to the floating hospital. The second wounds weren't as bad as the first ones, and the doctors did the same thing, stitched him up and sent him straight back to the hill with wounds that hadn't healed…and another Purple Heart to show for it.

I couldn't believe it.

"Mike! What the fuck are you doing back here?"

His body was covered with unhealed wounds, but he hadn't lost his arms or legs, so it was another Purple Heart and back to the hill. It would have been laughable—except it wasn't.

Not long after, my squad was sent out on a patrol from Hill 861-A to 861, and the NVA mortar and rocket fire was relentless.

Bbbbbooooom! Bbbbbooooom! Bbbbbooooom!

Guys were getting ripped apart left and right.

"Corpsman up! Corpsman up! Corpsman up!"

That's what we heard all over the hill, and it got in my brain that Mike had all of these stitches all over him and two Purple Hearts, and a third Purple Heart would be his ticket home.

I kept hearing explosions and Marines screaming, "Corpsman up! Corpsman up!"

I didn't plan it. I just grabbed my little can opener that we used to open our C-rations. It was about one inch long.

"Corpsman up! Corpsman up! Corpsman up!"

I wasn't thinking, really, and Mike wasn't looking. I took the razor blade part of the can opener and slashed it across his face.

Mike jumped, startled, and blood gushed from the wound.

"Corpsman up!" I screamed. "Corpsman up!"

Mike looked at me bewildered.

"If you're bleeding from incoming, it's a legal cut on your face, Mike! It's your third Heart! You're out of here, man!"

And that took him out of Vietnam. I took the man out of Vietnam.

We never talked about it afterward. He never said to me, "You know, Barry, you probably saved my life," or, "Thank you, Barry."

He wasn't trying to get out, but he wasn't upset with me either. It was a mixed blessing.

Mike spent all of his time in combat. He was a Marine's Marine, but that man was a magnet for shrapnel.

———

More than 58,000 Americans were killed in action in Vietnam, but many more were casualties of the war.

Mike Lucas had about a year and a half until his enlistment was up when he was sent back to the States and Camp Lejeune with his body riddled with shrapnel. He had metal floating near his spine when he was medically discharged from the Corps, and one piece was so close to his spine that doctors told him that sooner or later the metal would affect his spinal cord and he would lose the ability to walk.

Fortunately for him, that didn't happen, but his body bloated up and he became almost like a hermit. His legs became infected by Agent Orange and grew progressively more disgusting over the years.

Agent Orange was a herbicide, a defoliant that was sprayed from the air over huge areas of jungle and bush to kill all vegetation and deny cover to the enemy. It turned out to be deadly for many of those, friend and foe, exposed to it, even long after it had been deployed.

I didn't see him right before he died. He had moved to Florida, and we spoke on the phone several times a year for hours each time, but I didn't see him often. His legs got infected and he just let it go, let it get so bad that when he finally went into the hospital, he had death written all over him. He was only fifty-five, and doctors couldn't do anything for him.

He died on November 21, which is my daughter's birthday. November 22 is my birthday. Even though we didn't see each other much in the years after Vietnam, Mike was one of my best friends, the best man in my wedding. The bond always was there.

I came home from work the night Mike died and was eating dinner, just like any other night. Linda, my wife, stared at me. She had received the call from Lizzie, Mike's wife, and Lizzie told Linda that Mike had died. Lizzie had been Mike's high school sweetheart and they had been together since they were sixteen years old.

"What a blow," my wife probably thought to herself. "I have to tell Barry, and it's our daughter's birthday."

You know, when you lose a good friend, you don't want it to be on a family member's birthday, an occasion that you expect to be joyous. Linda waited until I had finished eating.

"I have something to tell you," she said.

"What?"

"Mike Lucas died today. Lizzie called me. They're not having a funeral. He didn't want one."

"Why didn't you tell me when I got home?" I snapped at her.

"I didn't want to upset you before you got a chance to eat."

Most of the conversations that Mike and I had after the war were about doing patrols out of Phu Bai and Khe Sanh. We really never talked about me giving him his third Purple Heart. He never said, "Well, Barry, thanks; you gave me my third Purple Heart;" or, "Barry, what the fuck did you do that for?"

Deep down, he knew it was a good thing. We just never discussed it. The bottom line was, he had no more control over what I had done than he did over the wounds he had received from the NVA.

He lived every day after Vietnam expecting that shrapnel to move near his spine and paralyze him. That's why his body bloated. He just didn't want to move, and it haunted him. He spent all of his time reading.

When Mike died, his body was riddled with Agent Orange… totally fucked up. He had huge sores all over his legs.

Mike Lucas got riddled with Agent Orange and died from it, and I wasn't affected by Agent Orange at all even though we served together almost the whole time. I can't question that. I can only hope to honor Mike and the rest of the fallen Marines in how I live.

26

Mail Matters

Our world at Khe Sanh was blood, death, and filth with deafening gunfire and blinding explosions as a constant soundtrack. Mail was our only link to the lives we left behind, the one that I left in those manicured subdivisions back in Long Island. For our families and friends back home, mail was their only way of knowing that we were still alive, or at least had been on the date of the postmark.

Mail brought comfort and confidence. Mail reminded us that beyond those bloody trenches there were still beaches and beautiful women and warm hugs and hot meals and people who meant more to us each day that we were lucky enough to still be alive.

"Will I ever see my parents again? Will I ever see my house again? Will I ever make it home?"

You think those things every day as a Marine at war. "Will I ever see where I grew up again?"

What the people back home think and feel may be even more horrible and helpless. Our minds were occupied at Khe Sanh by fighting for our lives. Those of our loved ones, though, could be tormented by worry and paralyzed by fear, and each day without mail grew worse.

———

I wasn't able to get mail out during the entire time that I was at Khe Sanh.

We were caught in the siege fighting every day; the shit was always hitting the fan. There was no way I could get mail out. When a chopper would come down, I would take a letter and just fling it on the helicopter and hope only that someone would pick it up from the deck as they were unloading the wounded and dead Marines.

I did that a number of times, and of course no letter ever made it home. Probably some guy stepped on them and ripped them and they just blew out of the helicopter.

Vietnam was a helicopter war, and those choppers were our lifelines at Khe Sanh. They were the main transports for men, food, ammunition, and mail. In the field, they represented the only way that we had of sending mail out and letting our families know that we still were alive.

Get in fast. Get out fast. That was the helicopter pilots' mantra.

But the NVA was right there. As soon as they saw a helicopter land, Ba-boom! Ba-boom! Ba-boom!

If Marines were wounded seriously enough, the choppers would take the risk and attempt to rescue them. But the choppers had to be fast, like ten seconds on the ground, maximum.

Boot camp drill instructors loved to say, "You've got ten seconds, and nine are gone!"

I don't think I appreciated the significance of that phrase until I carried wounded Marines to a chopper while the NVA hammered the landing zone with mortars.

One day, two of our guys got hit real bad. We carried them in ponchos to about one hundred feet from the landing zone. One guy grabbed a poncho by the feet and the other guy held it by the head and we picked up the wounded guys and ran to the Medivac chopper. We coordinated it so we got there just as the helicopter touched down.

I held one of the wounded guys by the head end of his poncho, making eye contact with him. Blood covered his body. How he was still breathing, I didn't know. He was turned inside out; all of his organs were exposed. But he was still alive, and his eyes fixed into mine.

"You're going to be fine; you're going back to the world," I told him. "Back home. You're making it back fine. You'll be fine. You'll be fine."

I really thought, "Just die already." The guy already was in shock, and there was nothing I could do.

The helicopters landed and four of us ran out with the two wounded Marines. We caught heavy fire: mortars and rockets.

The two guys carrying the first Marine went straight inside the helicopter. I was the last one on the ramp with the second injured man, and as soon as I got there, the pilot started taking off because shrapnel was riddling the helicopter. The cockpit windshield was a mess, and pieces of it protruded from the co-pilot's bloodied face.

I was barely on the ramp when the helicopter lifted, and next thing I knew, I was dangling from the ramp clinging to the poncho, and I couldn't reach anything else to hold.

I lost my grip. For one quick second, I opened my eyes and actually saw the tops of trees below me. I was falling from the sky, and the only thing I could think was that I was higher than the trees. I had enough time to tell myself to curl in a ball, like doing a cannonball at the swimming pool, and close my eyes and wait to hit the ground.

That's what I remember, falling, waiting, waiting to hit ground, waiting for the pain ...

I bounced. I swear, it was just like hitting a trampoline.

"What the fuck!?"

I had no idea what I'd landed on. The first time, I must've bounced ten, fifteen feet, but it felt like jumping out of a six-story building onto a trampoline: up three floors and down, and then up two floors and down, and then one.

My helmet flew off at the same time, and how I thought to do all of this, I don't know, but I tried to flatten myself out so I was not such an easy target for the enemy.

The NVA must've laughed their asses off.

"Look at that bouncing idiot!"

I was still wondering what I had landed on by the time I reached cover.

Well, for about six weeks, none of us had wanted to get our mailbags. The helicopters came and dropped the mailbags, but no one wanted to run out the one hundred feet under fire to get them. We had to get our ammunition and food, but screw the mailbags. We weren't about to get killed for mailbags.

So they piled up, and they may have saved my life. They must've been stacked four or five feet high and I landed right in the middle of them. That's why I bounced: those stupid mailbags that nobody thought were worth risking their lives.

Our three guys who got stuck on the chopper made it back the next afternoon while I was eating C-rations in one of the trench bunkers where we slept. They had assumed I was dead.

"We seen Fix get blown out of the helicopter! We seen Fix get blown apart!"

Their eyes had seen me fly out the back of a helicopter in mid-air while under heavy fire, so their brains assumed that I was dead.

"Yo! I'm fine!"

They almost jumped out of their skins.

"But we saw you get blown out of the helicopter!"

"That's right, but I'm right here. I'm good."

They said they were happy to see me, but they looked like they'd seen a ghost.

————

When we were able to get the mail, even the smallest surprises seemed large. The girlfriend of one of the guys in my squad wrote him a letter and put her pubic hair in the envelope. She probably sprayed a little perfume on it. He opened it in a trench bunker.

"Oh my God! I got pubic hair from my girlfriend!"

The rest of us scrambled for a look. "Oh shit! Let me see! Let me see!" We all passed around the envelope. There were twelve, fourteen of us, and we never took out the hair; we just looked at it in awe: little curlicues. Each of us took turns sniffing.

"Let me smell it! My turn to smell it! What a great girlfriend you have! My turn! My turn!"

That guy kept that pubic hair on him the whole time.

————

I never paid much attention to our mailman when I was growing up on Long Island, but we had the same one for years. He always saw us outside playing and watched me grow into a young man who joined the Marines and went away.

He knew that I'd been sent to Vietnam, so the first thing he would do each day was sort through his mail sack for any letters from me to my parents. They were easy to spot because they had "Free Vietnam" stamped on them. People in the military didn't have to pay postage.

The days that my letters did arrive, instead of putting them in the mailbox, he knocked on the front door and hand delivered them to my mother. It made his day, and he suffered along with my parents during the period when I couldn't get any mail out of Khe Sanh.

The only thing that any of them could think was that I was dead. When the siege broke and one of my letters finally arrived, he ran himself out of breath rushing it to my mother's door.

"Mrs. Fixler, I have a letter! I have a letter!"

He told me that story when I came home from Vietnam, and he shook my hand and said, "I have known you since you were a little boy, and I am very proud of you."

Letter carriers were invisible to me before then.

"Oh my God, thank you," I told him. "You're a stranger but you are not a stranger, and you really had heart for me."

My carrier wasn't unique.

My sister Vivian and I were close to my father's oldest sister, Aunt Helen, and Uncle Joe. They didn't have children of their own and treated us sort of as their surrogate kids.

They lived in a Miami Beach high-rise apartment, and I sent them a letter during the war, only I didn't have their apartment number. I just wrote "Aunt Helen and Uncle Joe" and street address on the envelope; no last names. I always only knew them as Aunt Helen and Uncle Joe.

The mailman there asked around the high-rise a little with no luck, and then, looking at maybe twenty floors of apartments, decided that he would knock on every door until he found them. And he did.

Those carriers went far beyond their duties to make sure that people received mail that the carriers knew was so important to them. Ever since Vietnam, I have held the people of the U.S. Postal Service in the highest regard.

———

Because of the mail situation, my parents didn't hear from me during that two-month period, and my father freaked out and got in touch with the senator asking for help locating his son.

I had made the mistake of mentioning Khe Sanh back when my letters were getting through, and then my parents saw all of the news from the siege. I didn't know that the world was about to blow up there, and my letter didn't get to my parents until February. By then Khe Sanh was receiving a lot of media coverage, and they had to read news reports like "26 Marines killed in Khe Sanh," so by the time they received my letter, all they knew was that was where I was supposed to be.

They tried, but it was impossible to find me. My parents couldn't get much information from the Marine Corps or from the New York senator, Senator Jacob K. Javits. My father was understandably upset, and he turned to a very influential rabbi who was politically connected.

My father did not say, "My son is at Khe Sanh."

He asked, "Rabbi, what's going on in Khe Sanh?" And the rabbi, very nonchalantly, said, "Looks like they're all gonna die."

My father collapsed. He got facial palsy. The muscles gave out from the nervous strain. He couldn't go to work for six months, and he never fully recovered.

My father never was warm to my mother's parents. His parents were warm and outgoing, and my mother's parents weren't, so my father never really took to them.

So no one knew what to make of it when my dad broke down crying at his father-in-law's funeral.

My father was a good guy, but he was pretty cold to my mother's family.

My mother was the youngest. She had three older sisters and three older brothers, and they all used to goof at my father.

He came out of World War II with nothing, and he was living off of slices of salami until he met my mother. He found out that her father was a jeweler and had a little money, and the story was that her father enticed my father to marry my mother.

"There is a little money in it for you. You marry my daughter, there is a little something in it for you."

It was the family joke: Louis Fixler married Ronnie Gerstel for the money.

My father was a gambler and a partier. Maybe my mother's family was a little bit too nerdy for him, a little bit too Jewish, a little bit too straight. They ran everything in their lives by the book and were as rigid as could be.

So everyone was bewildered when my father lost his composure during the funeral of my mother's father. Everyone knew he wasn't close with the in-laws, but he broke down crying during the services.

"Wow! This is a strange side of Louis, being so emotional," my oldest aunt told people, and she walked over to my father. "Louis, why are you crying? Are you that upset that papa died?"

"No!" he told her. "I'm crying because I may be standing here at my own son's funeral. He may be dead. He may not come back from Vietnam. That's why I'm crying!"

My aunt turned to him.

"Louie, I guarantee you, I say to you, your son will come home."

When I did come home my aunt told me the story.

"Barry, I've known your father for more than twenty years, and that was the first time I saw him cry, and he was crying because he was scared that you wouldn't come home from Vietnam. He thought that the next funeral was going to be yours."

27

Fatal Mistakes, Illusions of Calm

From my trench on Hill 861-A, I could see our concertina wire about ten yards down the hill, but very little beyond that. It was a week or two after we first were overrun, and we were holding our positions under the heavy fire.

The enemy would walk their mortars in our trenches, which were about two-and-a-half feet wide and stretched around the hill. We expected waves of humans to come at us at any moment. We'd been overrun before, and we didn't want that to happen again. We were getting shelled heavily by artillery and receiving mortars and rockets.

The fighting was so close and intense that it was incredible. We had to call in air support, and the NVA was positioned so close that the dirt and rocks from the explosions of our own bombs rained down on us.

We were fighting out of shoulder-deep trenches and had to duck our heads between bursts of fire, but if we ducked our heads the whole time, the enemy could just walk right up and say, "Now I got this hill." And our part of the hill wasn't very steep; pretty easy for the enemy to climb.

We had to have eyeballs outside there. We couldn't hide. I would pop up, fire, duck, pop up, fire, duck. The Marine sharing that section of the trench with me just stayed up firing away—boom! Boom! Boom! He wouldn't duck between bursts of fire.

His mentality was, "Fuck you, gooks! Come and get some!"

I ducked and he just exposed himself. A rocket must have hit the top of the trench right in front of us. The rocket acted just like a chainsaw and sheared the top of his head clean off right above the eyebrows. His nose was there, his eyes and eyebrows were there, but everything above was just gone.

I stared at him, amazed. Instinctively, he reached up to touch where his head had been, and then his body slumped to the ground. It must have been a reflex.

As he fell toward me, all I could see was that he had no head. His body was there, but no head, and all of his blood oozed toward me.

His uniform, and the skin on what was left of his face, seemed clean. I remember how odd that seemed because the top of his head was blown off, but there was no blood on him except on three fingertips on his right hand. Just the tips of the fingers, as if they had been dipped into a bowl of blood.

He just dipped his fingers in into his skull and fell and lay flat dead in front of me.

I still had to do my job, but I couldn't help looking back and forth at him between ducking and shooting. I kept seeing the blood flooding out of his skull toward me and soaking into the dirt, but continuing to ooze closer. But as fast as his blood flowed toward me, it was being sucked up by the dirt. It would flow and flow, and the earth kept sucking it up like a sponge.

It was as if red syrup spilled on the ground and it wouldn't stop flowing, like a stream coming toward me and seeping into the ground.

This was a guy I'd lived with for months, shared the same fox-hole with, and now he was dead on the ground in front of me and the top of his head was gone. I just stared.

Forty years on, I can't remember his name, but I'll never forget the blood flowing into the dirt.

———

On April 17, after seventy-seven straight days of incredibly tense, do-or-die fighting, the battlefield fell quiet at sunrise. Rockets, mortars, small arms and artillery had rained on us for more than two months. Now it seemed as if the NVA had just packed up and left.

That morning, instead of having incoming, incoming, incoming, there was calm, peace. No one screaming "Corpsman up!" We were thinking, "Oh my God, the NVA just left. We fucking won!"

A sudden feeling of relief and pride came over us: We won. We had just won the battle, so we took a group picture to show our defiance.

It's a great picture because if the NVA had seen us posing like that, all grouped, they would have lobbed everything they had at us. They would have said, "Wow, that's the best target in the world."

To me, the picture is a winning pose that symbolizes our victory at Khe Sanh, the moment we won. It's my personal Iwo Jima flag-raising photo. By grouping like that, and taking my helmet off, we were sending a message.

"Fuck you! We won!"

I was cocky and feeling sure of myself, so I pushed it to the next level. I took my helmet off. No helmet. You can see in the picture that most of the guys were so conditioned that they kept their helmets on. Me, I took off my helmet. "Fuck you!"

We actually celebrated by taking those pictures. The enemy wanted to knock us off that hill and couldn't. We were Marines.

We won. We felt ten feet tall. That shot is hanging on the wall in my office and I look at it every day.

Finally, another company of Marines came in by helicopter to take our positions. The thing that I remember most is the look in their eyes. We never exchanged words, but the awe in their eyes said everything.

"Wow, these are the guys, Echo Company. They've been through the shit. These guys are fucking bad, bad to the bone."

———

Later that day, we humped down from our hill feeling ten feet tall.

But very few of the guys in Echo Company who descended the hill were the same Marines with whom I climbed it seventy-seven days earlier.

I remember scanning the faces of the Marines around me, and I only recognized maybe a quarter of them.

As I kept searching those dirty, weary, war-hardened faces, it hit me: Most of my original Echo Company was gone. I'd climbed that hill with about 150 Marines, and I was still standing, but most of the men with whom I had entered the fight were either in hospital beds or dead.

Water had been so scarce the whole time we were up there that it was hard to resist when we reached the bottom and saw a stream. We were in a staging area near Hill 558 waiting for helicopters to come fly us out, and that stream was right there.

Normally, a corporal or staff sergeant would say, "Fuck the stream," if the people in charge felt that the area was still too dangerous. I'm always a cautious guy, and the higher-ups didn't pass the word down to stay away from the stream.

Deep down, I really felt that the NVA was crippled and had totally pulled out. It was that quiet. Normally, if the area were crawling with the enemy or if the commanders felt that the NVA might be massing for an attack, the B-52s dropped their payloads so close to us that we received the familiar dirt-and-rock showers.

We were never caught off guard when the friendly bombs fell close; we knew we were in imminent danger. That wasn't happening this time. We realized, "Whoa, this is the first freedom we've had."

The guys were excited by the prospect of drinking fresh water and washing up in a stream.

"OK," I told them, "you want water, you gotta have water."

I let my guys go. Two-man teams would go down to the stream and return all happy—"We got water, man!"—and then two more would go down. We dropped our guard, and then NVA rockets started screaming in. We didn't get any warning at all. Had they been firing mortars, we would've heard the popping sounds and taken cover, but there was none of that.

The NVA saw an opening and drew a bead on us, and they tore us to hell. Three corpsmen were killed. That's heavy. That almost never happened. The NVA had been watching us the whole time. We were totally ripped apart that day.

That was April 17, and I remember saying to myself, "What the fuck?!"

I had felt great, almost invincible, earlier that same day, and then to take a hit like that? It was a dramatic, emotional swing from one extreme to the other.

We erected this U.S. flag on Hill 861-A during the first day of the Siege of Khe Sanh.

Mike Lucas onboard the USS Repose receives a Purple Heart from a Marine Corps General. Photo courtesy of Mike Lucas' family

Weapons we collected from dead NVA soldiers on February 5, 1968, after they overran our position on Hill 861-A. Photo courtesy of Mike Lucas' family

I grin in the background as Mike Lucas, left, holds up three fingers to symbolize his third Purple Heart, which was his ticket out of Vietnam. The officer looking back at the camera probably didn't understand our excitement.

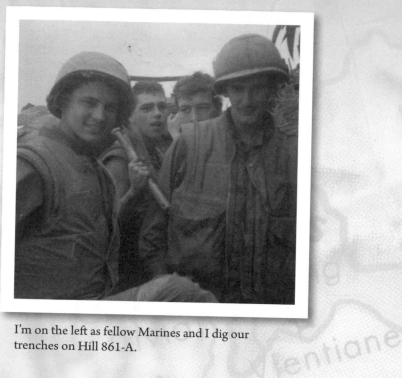

I'm on the left as fellow Marines and I dig our trenches on Hill 861-A.

A fellow Marine cuts my hair on the slope of a bomb crater on Hill 861-A.

The trenches that we clawed out of Hill 861-A were our main protection.

The Siege of Khe Sanh was near an end when someone snapped this picture of me in a trench on Hill 861-A.

Our trench line winds up Hill 861-A.

A helicopter carrying a mail bag approaches the
landing zone on Hill 861-A.

Hill 861 looms in the background as Marines relax in the trenches on Hill 861-A. The valley between the hills was infested with North Vietnamese soldiers.

I goof around with Marines James W. Heagy, left, and Jim Kaylor, center, during a lull in the fighting on Hill 861-A.

I'm at left with fellow Marines James W. Heagy, center, and Jim Kaylor, right, in a trench on Hill 861-A. Heagy later was killed during Operation Mead River. Kaylor, a Silver Star recipient, made it home alive.

I look up from a trench on Hill 861-A.

I'm without a helmet at the center of one of my favorite photos, which was taken on the day that the Siege of Khe Sanh ended. Grouping together to pose for a picture was our way of celebrating our victory while taunting the enemy.

NO SLACK FOR
A SHORT-TIMER

28

A Mixed Reward

I was formally promoted to corporal after the siege ended and we were evacuated to a huge Army base, where I was taking cover in a trench lamenting that we'd lost a reward meal of steak and eggs when NVA bombs followed us to the base.

Those of us who made it through that last harrowing attack near the stream at Khe Sanh were flown by helicopters to the base. The looks of awe in the eyes of the Army guys watching us exit the choppers pumped up our spirits again.

"Whoa! These are the Marines who just fought the Siege of Khe Sanh!"

Then orders came down that we were being freed from guard duty that night—the Army would watch the lines for us—and we all were to be fed steak and eggs.

"Fuck, man, this is great!" I thought. "Hot chow! Steak and eggs! The Army is going to watch the line, and they're looking at us like we're superhuman!"

I felt really good about myself and all the Marines of Echo Company, but it seemed as if the NVA really had it in for us. After we found our assigned positions in the line, we all headed to the mess hall for our reward meal. It was a *real* mess hall that served hot chow, and our steak and eggs were waiting.

I had just gotten my tray and settled down to cut into my

steak when NVA artillery ripped in from what seemed like every direction.

Ba-boom! Ba-boom! Ba-boom!

I swear that I was just about to cut into that steak, and the next moment, we were jumping up and knocking our trays over into the dirt and scrambling like madmen for our assigned spots in the trenches. There went our great meals onto the ground. I don't think a single Marine got to eat his entire steak and eggs.

"Damn!" we told ourselves. "There goes that! Back to fucking C-rations."

The Army guys probably blamed us for bringing the NVA artillery fire to the base with us.

It was a helpless feeling in the trenches with artillery rounds falling all around. I had no control. The next one could be a direct hit on me, and there was nothing I could do. But I was used to those conditions. It was *déjà vu.*

"Didn't we just do this at Khe Sanh?"

The artillery base was a maze of trenches about three feet deep with sandbags stacked to about shoulder height, and supplies and everything we needed were in the maze.

"Fixler! You're wanted in battalion command post!" another corporal ducked in and said to me.

"What the fuck?!"

The battalion command post was like the office of superintendent of schools, like I was in eleventh grade and the superintendent—not the principal—wanted to see me.

"Fuck. How do they know I exist?" I was low on the totem pole, only about eighteen months in the Marine Corps, and battalion headquarters wanted to see me?

Battalion headquarters was about five hundred square feet of bunkers, all Officer Country: lieutenants, captains, majors and lieutenant colonels who ran the show for a few thousand Marines.

So I ducked through the maze of trenches, artillery rounds hitting all over, asking directions every twenty feet or so until I found battalion headquarters. I wasn't some nineteen-year-old punk. I was a hardened combat veteran, and I felt like it until the major saw me.

"Lance Corporal Fixler reporting sir!"

I forget the major's name, but I figured the only two reasons he could have wanted to see me would have been if I had accidentally killed another Marine, or he wanted to put me in for the Medal of Honor. I didn't kill another Marine and I didn't rate the Medal of Honor, so I didn't know what to expect.

"You're Lance Corporal Fixler?"

"Yes, sir. I'm Lance Corporal Fixler."

"I have a combat meritorious promotion here from the headquarters of the Marine Corps in Washington, D.C., promoting you to corporal, but there's no way that I'm giving you this promotion!

"Good God, son, you look like you're fucking twelve years old. There's no way that one of my corporals is going to be twelve years old! Get the fuck out of here!"

He threw my promotion orders to the dirt floor. I bent down and grabbed them and left. The major had no choice. My promotion came from headquarters. So my reward for Khe Sanh was making corporal. Before that, corporals wouldn't look at me. A lance corporal couldn't even have a conversation with a corporal. Now I was a noncommissioned officer.

That was a big deal to me, and I felt great. It was meritorious, not a normal thing. Somebody higher up knew about me and really wanted to recognize me. I'd evolved from a raw, green Marine to a combat-seasoned corporal.

The major was still sputtering when I left.

"Fuck! I'm not going to promote a twelve-year-old. I am not going to have twelve-year-olds for corporals!"

29

Life-and-Death Decisions

Corporals ran the war in Vietnam. The responsibility for the guys in the field fell on them. Captains and sergeants didn't run the ambushes, the patrols. Corporals did, and on some occasions seasoned corporals deviated from the plan. I did once.

Second lieutenants didn't last long and didn't command respect. One time a second lieutenant came to me and said, "OK, your squad is going on a patrol tonight."

Then he took out the map and went over the details, the points where we were to check in and the times that he expected us to reach those points. Those were important details because our guys needed to have a good idea of where the patrols are at all times so they could direct artillery without friendly fire accidents. That was the idea anyway.

I was in charge of the map, and I had a radioman assigned to me. I was the senior corporal; it was my squad now, so I ran the patrols. But this other corporal was attached to our platoon and in my squad, and we looked at the map together and he said, "Fuck the lieutenant, man. This is impossible. It's suicide. No fucking way we can do this in daylight.... It's impossible at night."

We were on enemy turf and the terrain was terrible. It would be like walking through a swamp up to our necks with no light on. No light. We could at least do it during the day because we could see each other, but at night it was impossible.

The second lieutenant giving the order wasn't seasoned at all. He was going by the book. He was too new and too ambitious, and that's how mistakes get made. I couldn't say, "Lieutenant with all due respect, you don't know what the fuck you're talking about. This is a suicide mission."

So the other corporal and I decided that we'd just go right outside the lines and hang there and call in every half hour as if we were at our checkpoints.

"Fuck the lieutenant. He won't know."

We thought we had a good idea. Things don't always work out as planned.

We were right outside the wire, and things were going good. We called in every half hour as if we were at the checkpoints. The lance corporal on the other end kept telling us how the second lieutenant was really concerned that his mission be successful.

About 1:00 a.m., guys were getting a little restless. We started making too much movement. One of the lookouts inside the wire either saw us move or heard something, and they lit us up.

First they shot up illumination rounds, little parachute flares that stay lit for about fifteen seconds and turn darkness to daylight, and then mortars started exploding around us.

"Fuck, man!" I reached for the radio. I wanted to scream, "No, no! We're Marines! We're here! Fuck! No more! No more!"

I was that close to calling it off. I'm a good Marine, a very good Marine. If we had been caught, I would've been mortified, and I would have been reprimanded. I wouldn't want to think about the consequences had one of my men been killed. It would have been my fault, my responsibility if someone had gotten killed.

But they just sent out a few warning rounds. No one was hurt. I was so mad at myself for letting another corporal talk me into dodging a patrol, and I was so happy when 0600 arrived and the sun came up, and none of us were hurt. All of the guys thought it was great, like playing hooky.

———

Vietnam never let us relax. Right up to the end, things changed in a heartbeat.

I'd been through the deepest shit in Vietnam: Khe Sanh, Phu Bai, Quang Tri, Dong Ha. I wasn't the green Marine who stood and gawked at tracers flying past me. I was seasoned. I was up there in the pecking order. I had been twice promoted, and in a combat zone, from private first class to lance corporal to corporal. And now I was a short-timer, I'd be rotating back to the world in less than thirty days.

But instead of being more cautious, I let my guard down. I was too cocky, too confident. I started taking photos, clicking away with my camera while on patrol. It's not like I abandoned my M16 for a camera, but I was able to take a few snapshots, which would have been a no-no if there had been anyone senior to me in the platoon.

After a year in combat my attitude was, "Fuck it, man. I'm the senior guy in this platoon. I'm the most seasoned. I'm taking pictures. There's not one guy that can say to me, 'Hey, Fixler, don't take pictures.'"

That attitude almost caught up with me. I didn't want to get killed on my last patrol, but I couldn't look nervous to the guys in my squad.

"My time in Vietnam is coming to an end," I thought. "Let's get this combat operation over without anything happening."

We were on a sweep, a platoon-size operation of thirty-five to forty Marines. Search and destroy, flush out the enemy, engage. We were sweeping across an open, napalm-scorched field with waist-high elephant grass and shrubs.

The DMZ was the most dangerous area in Vietnam. It was a death land, no civilians around, so if anything moved it was kill first, ask questions later. And I was clicking away with the camera.

There was no way to see the two NVA dug into the ground just ahead of us. They knew we would be patrolling the area and had dug a little spider hole.

They waited until we were spread all around them, and then they both popped up from the ground and opened fire. I was maybe thirty feet from them, and bullets zinged all over the place. The NVA emptied their AK-47s and took off running in different directions.

I couldn't get a good shot because I had a Marine in front of me, and the last thing I wanted to do was shoot another Marine, so I held my fire. One of the NVA soldiers ran maybe forty feet before the other Marines cut him down with their M16s. He fell on the spot.

The other one got away. Not all of us could shoot or we would have taken each other out. The body of the first one was still jerking when we reached him. We didn't put a bullet in him because he was so riddled with bullets already, and he died maybe within a minute or two.

I didn't kill him; I was with the guys that killed him, but I'd seen my last enemy dead, so that was satisfactory. We almost didn't care about the NVA who escaped. We nailed the one guy, and none of us were hit. It was a good day.

———

After thirteen months of death and destruction it becomes very easy to kill. Pulling the trigger and taking enemy life is easy. Routine. But I never lost my sense of right and wrong. I never lost control. I didn't get to the point where human life meant nothing to me. It was just easy to kill the enemy.

One of the last ambush patrols I led was in bad, bad enemy territory, as usual. It was a night ambush from dark to dawn. There were no reports of friendly forces patrolling in the area. Anyone that walked into our trap was almost certain to be the enemy.

We set up in an area that had a great field of fire. It must have been pretty close to a full moon and the terrain was very advantageous to us for the ambush. We were totally concealed.

Somewhere about 1:00 or 2:00 in the morning, I saw five North Vietnamese soldiers approaching us, slowly. Everything moves slowly at night in the jungle.

They were less than one hundred feet from us. Perfect. I remember distinctly seeing the outline of their uniforms. I was analyzing them, watching and waiting for the right moment to cut them down. My rifle was on full auto. They were as good as dead.

Then something entered my mind…doubt. The headgear was similar. No friendlies should have been around. We were on enemy turf.

The decision on whether to open up on these guys was mine. I was the senior man; it was my ambush. I had the authority to kill anyone in the area.

The rest of the guys waited for me to fire the first shot. After the first round went off, it would have been a shooting gallery.

I stared at the silhouettes through the sights of my rifle. My thoughts raced. "Marines or enemy? Kill or let walk? Marines or enemy? Kill or let walk?"

Not easy decisions for anyone, much less a nineteen year old.

"Marines or enemy? Kill or let them walk?"

The silhouettes were sitting ducks. They would have had no chance.

"These are definitely the enemy," I kept telling myself, but that one percent of doubt kept popping in. All I had to do was squeeze the trigger and they were dead. They were almost certainly the enemy. But if that one in one hundred chance were right and they were other Marines, I would have been devastated. So I let them walk. I let them live.

Ask me forty years later, did I make the right decision even though in my heart I knew that they were the enemy? Absolutely.

30

Haunted by Horseplay

I'm proud that I made it through the war, went on with my life, and have been successful. I do keep a tough demeanor, but I was able to leave a lot of things behind in Vietnam. When you're just eighteen, nineteen years old and you've seen Marines get blown to pieces on a regular basis for thirteen months, your mind just kind of accepts it. It doesn't stick.

But a few months after Khe Sanh, something happened to a Marine that I could have stopped, and I carried that with me for years.

After Khe Sanh, we'd lost so many guys that we thought we'd be sent to Okinawa to regroup. Instead they sent us from the frying pan into the fire, Quang Tri Province, Con Thien and Dong Ha.

It was very close to North Vietnam and the NVA, and we were out in the field with no rear support. The only rear we had were the packs on our backs; we didn't have a combat base or outpost. We lived on the move, sometimes in helicopters but usually humping it on foot.

Every so often, we would come across a small outpost of Marines. It was usually planned, but low-ranking guys didn't know.

It was almost like R&R for us when we'd get to an outpost after humping for so many days and nights. Instead of sleeping in a little fighting hole in the middle of a field in enemy territory, we had sandbags, a wire perimeter and the extra protection of the other Marines that were stationed at the outpost. Still, the perimeter was small, usually only an acre or two.

Four guys shared a foxhole, and two guys were always on watch: on two hours, off two hours, 24/7. Two hours were pretty much the longest that we could sleep. This was war. Something was always happening or about to happen.

Our platoon had hooked up with another Marine company at one of these small outposts. We had a short break, maybe a few hours, before we had to saddle up for the next patrol.

As squad leader, my responsibility was to make sure half of the guys were always on watch.

We hunkered down in these protected bunkers that were roughly five feet wide and three feet high. The bunkers were covered with the same kind of perforated metal sheets they use to build combat runways, and sandbags were stacked on top of the metal sheets. They were always very crude, typical combat zone bunkers like the ones we built at Khe Sanh.

I had my back against the wall of a bunker. Two knuckleheads that were off duty for two hours were relaxing near me, and one had a revolver, an unmarked Smith & Wesson .38. He was telling the other Marine how his father was a cop and had sent the pistol to him in a care package.

He wore the revolver in a shoulder holster that stuck out from under his flak jacket, and the new staff sergeant had seen it a few days earlier.

This staff sergeant was the highest-ranking enlisted man in our company, and it was one of the toughest units in Vietnam. But he was new, and I was one of the most seasoned Marines by then.

"Fixler, I just came in. I know you've been shooting your way through all the battles and I respect it. You're one of my squad leaders. I respect you, but tell that fucking shit bird to fucking shit-can his revolver. Fuck! If he wants to carry more grenades, let him carry more grenades! If he wants to carry two M16s, let him carry two M16s! But no civilian weapons! That revolver is not military issue. Shit-can it! I'm telling you, man, get rid of it!"

The staff sergeant was a lifer. He had been in the Marine Corps for fifteen years, and he was strictly by the book. The revolver wasn't government issue, so as far as he was concerned, it was illegal. It had to go.

But the sergeant was not a combat-seasoned Marine. I remember he was kind of a slacker. I had overheard him talking with another sergeant, and the topic of conversation made me lose all respect for him.

The rest of us, the 26th Marines, we were seasoned and there were no slackers. We'd done the Siege of Khe Sanh and earned a major reputation for kicking ass. We had won one of the worst battles in Vietnam, and everybody respected that.

Walking away from the staff sergeant, I told myself, "Fuck man, I'm not saying anything. That Marine with the revolver would laugh at me. It's a weapon, and we're all here to kill. Screw it."

So I was in the bunker relaxing and the two knucklehead Marines were eating C-rations and talking about the revolver.

The next thing I knew, they started playing with the illegal handgun. One guy took the gun and emptied the rounds, then put one round back in and starting spinning the chamber, screwing around like a game Russian roulette. My eyes were still closed, but I listened to the knuckleheads. They were eighteen, nineteen years old, my age. We were all just knuckleheaded teenagers.

One guy—his name was Simpson—started baiting the other Marine with the pistol.

"You don't have the fucking balls to play Russian roulette. You don't have the fucking balls!"

"Fuck you," the Marine with the gun said. "I got fucking balls!"

"Oh yeah? Prove it. Pull the trigger!"

I just listened as they went back and forth.

"You don't have the fucking balls!"

"I got the fucking balls!"

"Fuck it," I thought. "They won't have the balls to do anything."

The Marine with the pistol spun the chamber and then snapped it in and pressed the gun to Simpson's neck. But Simpson wouldn't let up.

"C'mon, man! You don't have the fucking balls! Pull the trigger!"

"Fuck you! I do have the balls!"

"No you fucking don't!"

Simpson, he had everything to lose, nothing to gain.

"Let's see some fucking balls, man!" Simpson taunted him. "You ain't got 'em!"

BOOM!

"What the fuck?!" My eyes shot open.

Simpson had baited the Marine holding the pistol to his neck into pulling the trigger, and now Simpson's neck was gone, blown right out. I was lucky the bullet hadn't passed through and hit me. Blood was everywhere.

I didn't think they would actually do it. It was just talk. I should have said, "Fuck you, you're both jerkoffs! I got yelled at by the staff sergeant to make you get rid of that fucking revolver. Shit-can it, or hide it."

That's what I should have said. Part of me must have wanted to see if he had the balls.

BOOM and Simpson with no neck: That was my answer.

The bunker was tiny and it was a mess. Simpson's neck was all over it. His blood turned the dirt into sick mud.

I yelled, "Corpsman up!"

Then I grabbed Simpson by the legs. Someone joined me, and we dragged Simpson out of the bunker.

"Fuck! Fuck! Fuck! Fuck!"

A corpsman was right there and I left him with Simpson and returned to the bunker and tore into the PFC who shot him.

"Fucking goddammit, man! You fucking killed the guy! You fucking killed him!"

I ripped the gun from his hands. I was so pissed. I walked away from my area, and for the next two hours I wandered around venting, replaying the whole thing in my head. How could I lose a guy like that? How could someone survive Khe Sanh and get killed like that?

I decided I wasn't going to make it official that one Marine killed another Marine. I wasn't going to report it. I would catch hell for not taking the revolver from them. I had disobeyed a direct order by not making him throw out the revolver. It would go down however it went down, but I wasn't going to be the one to report it. The staff sergeant was waiting for me when I returned to my area.

"I fucking told you! I got fifteen years in this Marine Corps and I'm not going down! If I roll, you're fucking rolling with me!"

He was pissed. He even grabbed me by the collar. But by that point in my tour I was the man and nobody, not even a staff sergeant could intimidate me.

"I'm career, you stupid fucker!" the sergeant screamed. "If I roll, you're rolling with me!"

I was shook up about Simpson. The staff sergeant didn't bother me, though. My mentality was that he was the new guy, and we were getting killed every fucking day, fighting a new battle every fucking day. This wasn't Camp Lejeune or Camp Pendleton; this was war and we saw death almost every day.

So I didn't flip, really, and nothing happened. No one asked questions. Nothing happened. As far as I was concerned the PFC, the staff sergeant, Simpson and I were the only ones who knew, and we had a tacit agreement not to report the incident. The PFC and the sergeant weren't talking and Simpson was dead.

Later that day, we saddled up and moved on, never to return to that outpost. When you're used to seeing people get killed on a regular basis, you put it behind you quickly, and we did.

The chaos of combat, the daily grind and the stress of war buried the incident under more pressing matters. It was as if it never happened.

Well, not entirely. Not for me. I never forgot. Simpson got blown away, and I could have stopped it. I always felt responsible. Twenty-five years later, my wife and I were invited to a reunion in Washington, D.C. General Carl Mundy, who had been in Khe Sanh, wanted to honor my regiment, the 26th Marines, for its action at Khe Sanh.

It was nice to be acknowledged by the Corps, a great honor. The Marine Corps provided the transportation and food and paid for entertainment. They put on a whole ceremony with the "8th and I" silent drill team from Marine Barracks Washington, the oldest active post in the Marine Corps. It was a great honor.

I ended up mingling, running into guys I hadn't seen in twenty-five years, remembering some, acting like I remembered others. A Navy commander approached me.

"Barry Fixler?"

"Hey. How you doing?" I didn't recognize him.

"I'm your corpsman. I'm the doc." I still didn't really recognize his face, just maybe. The years had changed all of us, some more than others. That's why I don't really like the reunions.

He said he operated on so-and-so at such-and-such battle—so many firefights—and some of it sounded vaguely familiar. I wasn't sure.

He said the Navy had put him through college after the war, and he had just finished his twenty-five years as an officer. He was ready to retire. I still wasn't remembering him.

"I remember you and Simpson," he said, "the Russian roulette. You were his squad leader."

"How the hell do you know about the Russian roulette?"

"I was there," he said.

"No way that you were there! How do you know the story? No one knows the story!"

In my brain, there were only three people that really witnessed it, and I was the only one still alive. Simpson was dead, and the PFC who shot him got killed in combat a month later. The staff sergeant hadn't seen it and didn't report it. Other than me, no one alive really knew about it, or so I thought.

"I helped you drag him out. I'm the corpsman."

I hadn't really paid attention to the corpsman then, I had been so mad. We had just dragged Simpson out, and then I wandered off in a rage. I was so pissed, so fucking pissed.

"He's alive."

"What?" I asked.

"Simpson's alive."

"Impossible! His neck was wide open! I saw him die!"

"He wasn't dead. We medivaced him in two minutes. We got him to an aid station. He's alive."

I was stunned. For twenty-five years I had been carrying Simpson's death around with me. Not that I couldn't sleep at night, but

I never forgot. I had dragged his body out of that bloody bunker. Most of his neck was gone. I was sure of that.

"He couldn't walk or talk, probably still can't, but he's alive," the Navy officer said. "I followed him through. He spent three years in a VA hospital in Virginia. He wound up living in Virginia Beach."

Simpson actually ended up relearning to walk. He received one of those voice boxes that he used to talk. He was on disability and was always going to be part of the VA system, but he survived and could function.

I asked the Navy officer how to get in touch with Simpson; something compelled me. The ex-corpsman gave me Simpson's contact information.

It was about four on a Sunday afternoon when I called him, and Simpson's wife answered the phone.

"Who's calling, please?"

"This may sound odd or strange, but I'm his squad leader from Vietnam."

"Oh! You are? Honey, it's your squad leader, Barry Fixler, on the phone." She announced me like they had been expecting my call.

Simpson got on and we exchanged greetings.

"I gotta tell you that for twenty-five years, I thought you were dead," I said to him. "The corpsman just told me you're alive and gave me your number. What happened?"

He talked for a little bit about how he had recovered and moved on, but he sounded disconnected, distant. I asked him why he hadn't gone to the Khe Sanh reunion.

"I just didn't feel like it."

His answer was flat, emotionless.

"Are you pissed at me? You were in my squad when you got shot and I was your squad leader. Are you carrying a grudge on me?"

"No, I'm not pissed at you," Simpson said. "I don't carry a grudge."

"You know what? I'm glad you're alive. It's really great. I carried your death for twenty-five years and I do consider myself partially responsible. But you were eighteen. I was nineteen. I was only your squad leader because I had more time in Vietnam. But it was still my responsibility. I could've stopped you guys and I didn't, but I would like to see you and meet you at the next reunion."

He didn't seem very receptive. I knew that we would have no relationship.

We exchanged cordial goodbyes, and that was the last time we spoke.

At this point in my tour I was at the top of the pecking order. On combat patrols experience carried more weight than rank.

I make a muscle goofing with fellow Marines as we heated
C-rations while out in the field.

A tank guards a Marine outpost in Vietnam.

I sit front and center with a group of salty, battle-tested Marines on the edge of a bomb crater.

My face looks weary as I sit in a bunker at an outpost in Con Thien much like the one in which a Marine named Simpson had his neck blown out playing a game of Russian roulette.

The Marine at left watches for possible attackers during a search of a village suspected of being sympathetic to the Viet Cong.

Marines search for food and weapons in a village suspected of supporting the Viet Cong.

I prepare to leave on patrol. Each time my adrenaline flowed and pulse raced as I anticipated making contact with the enemy.

The terrain near the "D," our term for the
Demilitarized Zone, shows the ravages of war.

Marines gather around the body of a North Vietnamese
soldier that we killed in a firefight.

I am on a day patrol carrying all my war gear.

We traverse a napalm-scorched field during one
of my last patrols in Vietnam. Two enemy soldiers
popped up from the grass and attacked us. We
killed one of them, but the other one escaped.

We could feel the eyes of the North Vietnamese Army watching our every step on combat patrol near the DMZ.

I wear the look of "the man" as I relax after a successful patrol near the end of my tour.

I'm at back center with my hand on the shoulder of Ed Lutz as Joe "Cisco" Reyes keels directly in front of me. I gave him the nickname "Cisco" the day he reported to me as a replacement on Hill 861-A. I met Cisco again 43 years later at the Khe Sanh Veterans Association 2010 Reunion. Cisco is a retired police officer living in Texas with his wife. He has two daughters and two grandchildren. One of his daughters is a Marine.

Beer, always warm, was a rare treat, as the smiles on our faces testify after a successful combat patrol near the DMZ. That's me laughing at far right.

I'm at right with three of the Marines in my squad preparing to go on patrol.

Getting ready for another patrol near Con Thien.

My smile signals our return from a successful patrol.

I hold the skull of a North Vietnamese soldier at an outpost near Con Thien. We found the skull while returning from a patrol and thought that it would be cool to keep. The Marine at left was killed shortly after this photo was taken. The Marine at right later lost both legs in battle.

My salty combat boots tell you that I'd been in Vietnam long enough to command respect.

I shave on the bank of a river in Vietnam.

Bathing in a Vietnam mud hole was a rare luxury for us.

I pose with South Vietnamese soldiers.

It was on a truck patrol through a village like this where I saw a begging baby that made me so grateful for the prosperity that we enjoy in the United States of America.

Scarcity of water made brushing our teeth a rare luxury in Vietnam.
I'm on the left smiling and scrubbing.

I'm on the right and Larry McCartney holds a radio microphone at
center.

Joyner and I congratulate each other on officially becoming "short timers,"
which meant that we had fewer than thirty days left in Vietnam.

COMING HOME

31

Nothing Easy, No Parades

Mid-August 1968 was my time to rotate out of Vietnam and back to the States. In mid-July, Echo Company was ordered to a Navy ship to train for a special combat landing technique.

I only had thirty days left to do in country, so I was excluded because it would've been pointless to train me for a mission that I wouldn't be there for.

I didn't know it then, but I got lucky. That special Echo Company mission took place three weeks after I rotated back to the States, and about half of the Marines in my old squad were killed. The incident is known as LZ Margo.

Instead of the training, I was sent to another unit, Third Battalion, Third Marines, Headquarters and Supply Company 33, and I received major respect when I reported.

"Hey, brother, you've been in the shit for a long time."

My new company, H&S 3/3, went out on missions like everyone else and took casualties like all other Marine companies, but they intentionally kept me behind the lines because I was a short-timer.

As it turned out, my biggest danger was the food.

I had been in combat for so long eating nothing but C-rations

189

that they were all my stomach would accept. The steady diet of hot chow at the base made me sick. I had already missed one flight date back to the States over reporting technicalities, and I would've missed another one, but the guys did a very cool favor for me. Very cool. I had a terrible fever, sick as could be, and if I had gone to the infirmary, I would have missed the next flight date.

The base wasn't immune to the war; we caught NVA artillery fire all of the time. I really was afraid that, after all of the shit that I had been through, I would get killed on an infirmary cot.

I was delirious with a fever and I couldn't even stand, but the guys respected me as a Marine and for what I'd been through, and they hid me on a cot in a hooch where superiors couldn't see me. They would sneak me in to get shot up with whatever medicines might help me and didn't report any of it.

We had to make formation for two roll calls a day, and I was just too sick. But whenever my name was called—"Corporal. Barry Fixler!" —one of the guys would yell, "Here!"

I got away with it. They got away with it.

Things were dicey to the very end, though. My flight date was August 22, 1968, and the night before, we took very heavy artillery fire.

Ba-boom! Ba-boom! Ba-boom! Same old Vietnam.

Then we got word that it was our own artillery, friendly fire. Our guys were targeting an area just outside our lines where a fire-fight was happening, but their rounds were coming up short.

"Fucking great," I thought. "I shouldn't even still be in Vietnam, and now I gotta get fucking killed by friendly fire. What a fucked-up way to die."

Oddly enough, I don't remember leaving Vietnam the next day. I don't remember saying goodbyes or getting on the plane, or the flight from Vietnam to Okinawa.

Maybe a part of me didn't really want to leave. I knew that I would miss the combat, the excitement, the danger. I would never again experience the intensity of combat, or so I thought.

———

The plane flew us from Vietnam to Okinawa, which was where they had told us as green Marines a little more than one year earlier that our odds of getting out of Vietnam alive and intact were only about one in three. If we weren't one of the lucky ones, we were dead or severely wounded.

All I had leaving Vietnam was my green fighting uniform because the NVA had blown up our main supply. I had lived in it for many months, and it was really salty. Saltier meant cruddier, and cruddy showed that you had a lot of time in the bush, so that was a badge of honor. I'd been through the shit. If your uniform was all nice and starched, you were a child.

I was on the flight from Okinawa to the States with maybe one hundred other Marines when a captain stood up in front of us. I was feeling about ten feet tall. I had survived everything that they threw at me, and I was whole, physically and mentally.

"I know you Marines are feeling great about yourselves," the captain said, "but all of you are coming home from your first tour. This was my second, and I can tell you right now that back home, nobody cares what you did in Vietnam. Nobody cares that you just fought a war, that you risked your life. Nobody cares. The only people that care are your mother, your father, your sister and your brother. That's it."

No parades, no pats on the back. The public was not going to run over and say, "Yay! You're back from Vietnam!"

That disappointed me probably more than it surprised me, and I was apprehensive about what home would be like.

———

As the next few years unfolded, Vietnam wasn't a popular topic, and I never really talked about it. The only ones I would really talk about it with were other Marines. We'd laugh and talk about experiences to which people who weren't there just can't relate.

It was almost too far-fetched to try to explain Vietnam to somebody who didn't experience it. Even talking with an Army guy who had been there wasn't right. It had to be another Marine.

It was probably twenty to twenty-five years down the road that things opened up a little bit and people would ask me about Vietnam. Not that it bothered me. I was very busy with living in the present: working, going to school, having a family, improving and enjoying my life. I was very ambitious, very busy.

But it's important to talk about combat experiences. To the guys coming back from Iraq and Afghanistan today, I say—be proud. Be proud that you killed the bad guys. I understand feeling bad about colleagues who died, but the guys who were killed and maimed would want you to go on with your life in a very positive mode. I believe that the guys that I was with, if they could talk from the dead, they'd say: "Don't even dwell on me, man. I'm dead. You made it out. Enjoy life."

Me, I enjoyed the Marine Corps. I loved the discipline, the camaraderie.

Even after I finished my military commitment I volunteered again in the active reserves.

———

I was rare for a reservist, having already survived combat. Maybe only 20 percent of reservists were combat veterans, and we were given respect from active duty Marines that non-combat reservists weren't.

Every summer we had to spend time in specialized training… desert training, amphibious training and so on. For amphibious training, we were sent to Little Creek, Virginia, and integrated with regular forces.

I enjoyed being with the fellas. I enjoyed the adventure. I could get up in a heartbeat at 4:30 in the morning and put on a field pack and just go. I fed off of it.

At Little Creek, we were ordered to perform a staged beach landing for a slew of civilian visitors, VIPs and dignitaries. We weren't on a beach, but on dry land, a demonstration area as big as several football fields. The crowd sat in bleachers facing the fields, and the officers spoke with their backs facing us.

They had us put on all of our war gear and pack into these landing craft that were left over from World War II. Each craft held about 160 troops, and we were supposed to charge out of them toward the crowd at the command of the colonel presiding over the demonstration, and we were told to be organized, enthused and intense.

We all thought it was bullshit, a dog-and-pony show that made no sense. The landing craft were old wooden pieces of crap that had been made permanent parts of the training grounds. We were supposed to charge out of the landing craft, stay organized, run and drop to a prone position with rifles shouldered, look menacing and impress the crowd. But our attitudes about the whole deal weren't good. They were poor. It was just stupid to us.

"This is bullshit," we thought, "dumb to do this for civilians. We know how to do this. There's nothing in it for us."

The officers could tell.

"Look, Marines, don't embarrass us," they said. "Don't just la-de-da walk off the beach and run a little bit and fall down. Look like Marines! Be motivated! Be Marines!"

But we just looked at each other thinking, "What the fuck? We gotta show off to these civilians?" We were pretty half-assed as we packed ourselves into the landing craft. I was in the craft that was supposed to empty first.

He was supposed to give the hand signal, and our mission was to charge and look organized. My craft was supposed to empty first, and the Marines in the other craft were to follow our lead.

What we didn't realize was that those old wooden landing craft had been sitting in that field forever, since WWII, and there were huge swarms of hornets nesting in the back. Fucking hornets. The back of our craft was filled with them, a big swarm from a huge nest that they'd probably been building for twenty years.

We'd packed ourselves in backwards, so that we were facing the ramp that would open for us to storm out, and when the guys in back finally were pushed up against the hornets' nests, the bugs got mad. There must have been thousands of them, and they attacked us full fury before the officer ever gave the hand signal to charge.

The officer was still on the podium explaining to the civilians and dignitaries packing the bleachers what was about to happen.

"On my command, you will see a full battalion of gung-ho Marines…"

But that was as far as he got. The hornets were stinging us like mad, and we just blew out of the craft screaming, waving our arms in the air and running like fucking madmen.

It worked out perfect. The officer thought that he'd accidentally given the signal early, and that we were the most motivated Marines in the history of that demonstration.

The guys in the other craft had been bitching just as much as we had about how stupid the whole thing was, but they saw us storm out and thought, "Whoa, look at this! They're taking it serious! They're gonna make us look bad!"

So they ran and screamed like madmen, too. The officers probably thought that they hadn't seen Marines so intense and motivated since Iwo Jima. They had no way of knowing about the hornets.

32

Stresses from War

Some people can put war behind them and get on with their lives. I'm one of those who could. Others never get over it. We have a term for them: "vetted out." Smiley Jones served with me in Echo Company. Smiley was all vetted out.

My squad leader, Tom "Ike" Eichler, organized a parade for Vietnam veterans on June 13, 1986, in Chicago. He became a Chicago police officer and a big organizer of veterans.

A year before, on May 7, 1985, New York City had held a parade for Vietnam veterans. I was psyched up that day, and I ran into Smiley again.

"Man, they're acknowledging us for the first time." I was so proud, happy and excited that I decided to blow off work. "Fuck it, man! This is my day! They are honoring not just me but all the Viet vets!"

The parade started on the Brooklyn side of the Brooklyn Bridge. I was so psyched that I got up early and started walking to the bus terminal to get into the city. I needed to get one bus into Manhattan, then another one to Brooklyn.

It was 6:30 in the morning, and I didn't have to be there until 8:00 or 9:00, but I was anxious and wanted to be a part of everything.

Normally I would take a bus into the city, but I was so excited when I reached the bus stop that I just stuck my hand out to hitch a ride.

Sure enough, a guy stopped at the light and offered me a lift.

"I'm a Viet vet and they're having a parade for us," I said. He took me exactly where I needed to go. Thousands of Vietnam veterans were already at the staging area, and the media was all over the place. It was a big deal.

Everyone was getting organized. Army Airborne people were looking for others who were Army Airborne. Then they'd try to find their units. So it was Cavalry looking for Cavalry, Marines First Division looking for First Division, Fifth Division for Fifth Division, and so on. People held up signs saying which units they were with.

Finally, I saw Khe Sanh veterans. That was me! There were several of us, and I hoped I would see someone from my company. Sure enough, I saw Smiley, Echo Company. We hooked right up. "I did this; I did that," just shooting the shit and catching up.

Now, Smiley is a great guy, but he was all vetted out. He was heavy set, muscular and wore combat gear. His front teeth were missing. … He was just vetted out.

"What the fuck's with you?" I asked him. "No front teeth?"

"Oh, I get in fights all the time," he told me. "Last Friday night, I got slugged with a pool stick." Another time, he was working pumping gas and said something to a customer and the guy bashed him in the mouth with a tire iron.

"I decided I'm not putting my teeth on anymore."

"That's good, Smiley," I said. "I agree with you." 'Cause he got in all these jams, right?

We marched together. We went over the bridge and down Wall Street and office workers threw confetti from the buildings. It was the first time that our country had thanked us for fighting in Vietnam. Smiley and I bonded again, and we kept in touch.

The Chicago parade was on June 13, 1986. A few weeks prior, my old squad leader Ike called me. He was planning a get-together with Khe Sanh veterans at his house the night before the parade and wanted me to come. I invited Smiley. I had money and he didn't, so I offered to pay. I was excited and I wanted him to be there. Smiley kept thanking me.

We left New York on a Friday, and Smiley met me at my office in the Empire State Building. It was a normal, conservative office where everyone wore business clothes.

I was just working as usual when one of my secretaries ran in with a panicked look on her face.

"There's a madman out there and he says he knows you!"

I looked out and saw Smiley. He wore combat fatigues with combat boots, a floppy hat and no front teeth. I could almost picture camouflage paint on his face.

The women in the office couldn't believe that I in my business suits could have a friend like Smiley.

"He's fine, absolutely fine," I assured them, but they seemed skeptical.

Our flight was on People Express Airlines, that no-frills, low-budget carrier that Continental bought out in 1987. We arrived a little late and ended up with seats on the second-to-last row.

I sat by the isle and Smiley sat next to me, and this poor kid, who was maybe twenty years old, was stuck by the window. I looked like a businessman. Smiley looked like he'd just walked out of the jungle with no teeth.

We hadn't been in the air long and I was half-dozing when Smiley pulled out this big fucking pipe. It looked like one of those old fetish Indian peace pipes, a long, old pipe with leather tassels and feathers and everything, and he started packing it with marijuana.

You could smoke cigarettes in the backs of planes in those days, but this was different. I just watched him, too stunned to do anything. He packed the pipe with pot and lit it.

"I don't fucking believe what's happening here," I thought.

In Smiley's mind, he was a Vietnam veteran and sort of above the law.

"Oh fuck!" I thought. "There's no way that I'm going to jail with this guy. There's fucking no way."

I didn't say to him, "Are you out of your fucking mind?" I just told myself, "You know what? He's a big boy and whatever goes down is going down."

I got up and walked to the front of the plane where they had the magazine racks. Smiley was about 6-foot-2, 270 pounds, and that kid was still pinned between him and the window when Smiley fired up the pipe. All the poor kid could do was slump as low into his seat as he could and pretend he was asleep.

A cloud of pot smoke rose from the back of the plane, and the more Smiley puffed, the more smoke drifted toward the front. The cabin reeked of marijuana.

As the cloud of pot smoke grew and drifted further up the plane, I could see the passengers sniffing around, as if they were thinking, "What the fuck is that?!" Then they would turn their heads around and see Smiley, this big fucking madman wearing combat gear and no teeth and smoking away on this big peace pipe stuffed with weed.

The stewardesses wouldn't even walk back there. They looked at him, and, holy shit, he didn't look normal. They were afraid he'd chop off their heads.

I stayed up front for a good half hour until Smiley finished getting stoned. I imagine all the people around him were pretty high, too. The plane was a big stink bomb, but everyone was too scared by Smiley's appearance to do anything.

I was pretty sure that cops were going to storm the plane when we landed in Chicago, and I was ready to tell anyone who would listen that I had nothing to do with him.

But it didn't happen. We all tiptoed off the plane, but the only cop waiting at the airport for us was Tom. He and a few other Vietnam vets were there to greet us and give us a ride.

"You won't believe this," I told Tom. "The whole way over here, this guy was smoking pot. You're a cop, man! He didn't get arrested?! They didn't call in the federal agents?"

"Naw, nothing," Tom said.

"Holy fucking shit! Jesus Christ almighty!"

We all broke down laughing. How the hell could someone smoke pot in a public airplane in front of everybody and get away with it?

Smiley couldn't have cared less. He was at a stage in his life where he thought, "Done this, done that. So they fucking put me jail? I've been to jail. You know what? I have nothing more to give and nothing to lose."

That was his attitude.

———

I don't believe in Post-Traumatic Stress Disorder. I saw combat, saw people die horrible deaths, and I made it through, counted myself lucky and came home and went on with my life. But I know other veterans have had far different experiences, and my position isn't politically correct.

In 2007, Rockland County was looking for combat veterans to counsel veterans coming home from Iraq and Afghanistan who had Post-Traumatic Stress Disorder, so they reached out to me, probably because I'm well known locally for supporting our troops.

"This is a great idea," I thought. "I'll go for it. Maybe I can help them."

I spent the whole summer taking classes. I closed my store early every Monday for months. I figured it was worth it to help other vets. I was in for an awakening.

The counselors teaching the classes were all women in their fifties and sixties, and they were very sympathetic. Their training was in domestic situations, spousal abuse, and things like that. Speaking to fresh combat veterans was new for them, and I disagreed with everything they said.

Everything was too soft, too simple and too easy. I went ahead with it, but by the end of the classes, we all knew that I was not a guy they wanted as a counselor. They didn't assign me any veterans when the course was over. Zero. They knew my attitude was sort of tough.

The instructors would say things like, "Don't cross your arms; you're showing bad posture. If you show bad posture, you're showing something that's negative. They think that you're the counselor and you're supposed to make them feel good, and if you make them feel bad, they could go home and kill themselves because of a bad counseling session they had with you."

They figured I was the right guy to push them over the edge, so that was the end of that.

In March of 2008, the woman who runs the local program put together a lecture and book signing by Dr. Edward Tick, who wrote *Healing Our Nation's Veterans from Post-Traumatic Stress Disorder*.

About one hundred people showed up at the New City Library, men and women veterans from the Iraq war all the way back to World War II. It was about fifty/fifty men to women, not all veterans. Some were sons, daughters, parents—people who had some connection with veterans—and a lot of the people in the audience were civilians with no military connection.

I went. I know how I feel about Post-Traumatic Stress Disorder, but I wanted to hear what the other side had to say. I said to myself, "Barry, just keep it low key and listen. Just sit there and be quiet."

Tick started talking about how the ancient Greeks and Romans acted toward their warriors when they returned home from battles. He didn't say "veterans;" he said "warriors," and he carried the point through the centuries to the American Indians. The warriors would fight to protect the tribe, and the tribe would give them the highest respect and special treatment because they had defended the village.

He was only ten, fifteen minutes into a two-hour lecture, and he started describing one of his patients who had fought in the Siege of Khe Sanh. He described how traumatized the Marine was, how his hill was overrun, how he had to kill or be killed, how his life was torn apart, how he lost his soul right then and there.

It was obvious to me that Dr. Tick was describing the night of February 5, 1968—the night we were overrun on Hill 861-A.

Tick was quoting his patient, speaking for the Marine now: "I lost my soul! My life is gone! Everything is gone! I can't continue! I can't fight! I can't do anything!"

People sat with their mouths open in awe, listening to Tick talk about this so-called warrior who lost it all, lost his soul, everything, died, spiritually died at that point, and I couldn't keep quiet any longer.

"Barry…" I warned myself, even as I watched my hand rise. This was a lecture. He wasn't expecting questions, but I caught his eye from the rear and he acknowledged me.

I stood and introduced myself.

"I was at Khe Sanh. I have credibility, a Unit Citation from President Lyndon B. Johnson. And I was on that hill, at that exact place, at that exact moment. If what that Marine said to you about losing his soul and losing his life, losing everything, if he had said that to me then or now, I would say to him, 'You are a coward!'"

Then I sat again. The room was silent. Tick lectures for a living—he's a professional—but he struggled to regain his composure.

"I see your point," he mumbled. "I see your point."

But I threw him off. What were the odds? Only a few hundred men actually were at Khe Sanh and on that particular hill on that particular night, and here one was in New City, New York, messing up his lecture, and there was no way he could challenge me.

All the veterans—guys from Iraq, Vietnam, Korea, and World War II—watched me as I sat. So did three cadets from West Point. I found out later that they were on assignment, researching Post-Traumatic Stress Disorder. Some of the other veterans spoke, and their experiences were different from mine. They came back from Vietnam and were spit on by anti-war protestors, treated horribly, and they were affected.

I didn't get any parades, but nothing negative, either. I went on with life, and I was very proud of my service.

Parents, family, close friends––they were the only ones who really cared about the veterans. The country usually cares about veterans in passing, but America was turned around during Vietnam. People were negative about the war.

I kept my peace and let the other veterans speak for the rest of the lecture, until one of the West Point cadets stood and asked Tick, "What can we do to stop this PTSD?"

I blew it then. She asked Tick the question, but I popped up.

"That's easy. Are you guys trained to get used to seeing bodies scattered all over the place? Well, when we kill a bad guy in Iraq, when we blow their skulls apart, we should freeze that body and send it to West Point and scatter it around so you can smell the blood and the horror and get used to fighting that way. If you're used to fighting with blood and dead Iraqis all over the place, it will be nothing. That's what needs to be done. Period."

Everyone was quiet again. I glanced at the three West Pointers. Their eyes were wide, mouths still, like "Whoa!" I got that look from some of the others in the crowd, too.

But after the lecture was over, the lady who coordinated the event came up to me.

"Barry, you nut! You crazy nut! You're a lunatic! Barry, you're a lunatic!"

But she said it laughing, and she hugged and kissed me.

"I'm not in trouble?"

"Come to my office, but don't talk crazy like that," she said. Dr. Tick was going to be there, selling and signing his book.

We milled around outside her office and a few people came up and told me they'd liked what I had said.

The way that she said "crazy," I didn't take it personally. Just like during the lecture, when Tick said someone who didn't come back from war with Post-Traumatic Stress Disorder had to be a psychopath or a sociopath, a nut. I don't remember which word he used. He wasn't talking directly to me, and I didn't take it personally.

He said someone who goes off to war and kills, and then returns and lives as if nothing ever happened, had to be a psycho or sociopath. I just laughed.

I had a chance to talk with Tick about Khe Sanh. He didn't have any animosity toward me. He understood. War affects people differently. Some are like me. They go on. It tears others apart.

I always thought my reaction was normal. I can only speak for Marines in my generation. I'd say 99 percent of Marines that would come back from war would get busy and move on with their lives. And those that didn't, the ones with mental problems, some of them may have had problems before they went to war.

Dr. Tick signed his book *War and the Soul* for me:

"For Barry, Your soul has seen and survived hell in the raw. Thank you and bless you for your service and sacrifice. I honor and salute you. Welcome home. Ed Tick."

33

Real Homecoming

I was pretty sure in 1968 that God gave me a personal welcome home from the war.

I wasn't the school kid that left a year and a half ago. I'd been to Parris Island, Lejeune, Pendleton, Okinawa and war. War. I'd just done thirteen-and-one-half months in Vietnam. I'd seen horrors, but I felt great about myself.

Now I was home on a twenty-day leave, my first leave after returning from Vietnam. I was alive, I had all of my body parts, and as boys will do, I went looking for girls.

There were a lot of Irish pubs in Syosset where we used to hang out when I was a senior in high school. So I went to one of those Irish pubs on my first Friday night home and I hooked up with a girl that was perfect for me.

She was a pretty, blonde, Irish girl with big tits who had just graduated from high school. What luck! I couldn't believe it! She was the perfect one, and she wanted me to come to her house!

The only problem, she lived with her parents. But her parents weren't home, she said. They wouldn't be home until 2:00 in the morning and it was only about ten o'clock.

I almost had to pinch myself. In high school, it would take months and months to get laid. My tongue would hang out. Now, man, I was in her house and she was leading me to her room...and I knew what was next!

"This is the greatest," I thought.

We were having sex, and all I could think was that I was getting a personal gift from God because I had endured the hardships of war, protected America and killed bad guys. I really thought that. God was rewarding me!

Her house was a split-level, like the one I grew up in, with all the bedrooms upstairs, and one staircase right next to the front door. Her front door was already open before I even knew what was happening.

Her parents were home!

"Oh my God! My mother and father are home! My mother and father are home! Get under the bed!"

I scurried under the bed while pulling on my pants. I'm still not sure why I didn't bolt. I squeezed under the bed with half of my clothes off, thinking, "Run? Stay? Run? Stay?"

I probably would have given her father a heart attack. She'd turned her light on—to make things look normal—and her dad walked in her room.

I was squeezed under the bed with my head half-stuck watching his shoes go back and forth. I still debated running, but it wasn't that simple. I didn't know what clothes I had on, and I couldn't remember where the door was. I couldn't tell from her dad's shoes how big the guy was. Would I have to fight him?

I just knew she'd be punished for about forty years, so I held tight. Dad sat down on the bed, and I had to listen to what seemed like an hour of father-daughter small talk. He had no idea that I was there. Maybe it was only five minutes, maybe fifteen, whatever. Here I was a Vietnam veteran, pinned down by father-daughter talk.

He finally walked out of the room and we just waited about an hour for her parents to fall asleep, and then I got the hell out of there.

Marines who come home on leave only have so much time, ten, twenty days, so they can be pretty much one-track. I was: girls, girls, girls; get laid; get laid; get laid. That's all my brain would register.

I had my father's car, a big Pontiac Catalina, '67 or '68. He always bought big American cars. His Catalina was a four-door sedan, the biggest one they made, a boat. It was a family car, a father's car, definitely not cool. In those days, they had big, heavy, metal bumpers.

And God was still giving me treats because I hooked up with a totally different girl, a dark-haired beauty. It was too easy, nothing like before I left for the Marines.

"How can we treat Barry? Let's give him two different girls!"

The girl and I went bar hopping until around midnight.

We were just driving around the developments on Long Island in my father's Catalina. The radio was playing, I was kissing her, and next thing I knew, her hand was on my lap.

ZIPPP!

And then she leaned over.

"Thank you God! Thank you God! Thank you God!"

I couldn't believe it. No effort. I didn't do anything. It was as if God just said, "Okay, whatever two girls Barry wants, he's getting."

It was so perfect.

You know how sometimes you can remember where you were, what you were doing, the first time you heard a song? Right then was the first time I heard The Beatles' "Hey Jude."

The song had been out for a while, but I had been in Vietnam, so first time that I heard it was home on leave from war.

"Hey Jude" and fooling around with a pretty girl while I drove my father's Catalina around these rows of Long Island houses at

1:00 or 2:00 in the morning. Everyone asleep. Lights out. Real quiet.

Some things you never forget.

"La la la, la-la la la, la-la la la, Hey Jude…"

BOOM!

Fucking BOOM! I smashed the car!

La-la la la!

I probably was only moving about ten or fifteen miles an hour, but I ran right into a parked car and smashed in its side.

God was still smiling on me, though because neither of us got hurt. The parked car was a different deal.

"Shit!"

I cut the lights, backed up, drove out of there and took her straight home.

My father's car had to be messed up, too. Not that he would've freaked. He wasn't that type. As long as no one got hurt, he couldn't have cared less. But I felt bad. I thought that I'd smashed up my father's Catalina.

But that was the thing about those old Pontiacs. They were built like tanks. I got the car home in the garage and there wasn't a scratch on it. Nothing, just another gift from God.

34

'Stay Cool! Mitch'

"Stay cool! Mitch"

That's how Mitch Sandman used to sign off the letters he sent to me in Vietnam, and I felt the void of his absence as soon as I returned to the States.

Mitch and I became buddies in second grade, and that was that; we were tight from then on. I went off to the Marines and he started working and going to school at night, but then he was drafted, and the war decided our fates.

If you lived in Long Island, in Nassau County, in the 1960s, you couldn't drive until you were seventeen years old if you took driver's education, or eighteen if you didn't. But Suffolk County was just a few miles east of us, and you could get a junior license in Suffolk and drive at sixteen. So when we turned sixteen, our parents would drive us over to Suffolk County to get our junior licenses.

We were sixteen when Mitch convinced his father to get an old jalopy, a 1951 Ford, for $50. It was a hunk of crap.

My family had new gardeners and after school I started working for the gardener. Not that I needed it, but it was a challenge for me, so I started working for him after school and on Saturdays. Somehow I brought Mitch into this, and he came and took things to another level.

He had this piece of crap old Ford, and Mitch said, "You know, Barry, over in Hicksville there's a house that's selling a bunch of shrubs, and we could just hop the fence and pick some shrubs and we'll give them to our gardener."

What Mitch was talking about was probably a nursery or something. It was a school night, about eight or nine o'clock, and we weren't supposed to be driving in the first place. His car had no license plates, no insurance, nothing.

Mitch and I jumped the fence at the Hicksville place, took about six little shrubs and put them in the back seat of his car. We shot down to where our gardener guy was and we put the shrubs on the back of his truck and drove back home.

The next day, the gardener said, "How the fuck did these shrubs get on my truck?"

But, hey, it was free merchandise, so he sold it.

A few days later, we did the same thing: hopped the fence, lined the shrubs in Mitch's back seat and then drove them over and put them on the gardener's truck. The gardener loved it. He sold them to all of my neighbors.

Mitch and I laughed. The guy probably thought, "I dunno where they're coming from, but I'm not asking because I'm making a lot of money."

He wasn't paying us a thing. I never needed the money. We just did it for the thrill.

"Wow, look how nice those look all lined up."

We were having a great time.

Then one night we jumped the fence and all of a sudden, a big guy came out screaming like a son of a bitch.

"I'm gonna get you guys!"

We jumped in the car, but the guy jumped in front of it, so Mitch made a U-turn onto the lawn and we drove away, but the guy ran to his pickup and chased us.

He followed us through this subdivision, and we were thinking we were about to get beaten when I got the idea to start tossing the plants. I started tossing the plants out and they hit the street, wobbled and then popped straight up because of the big root balls. In no time there was a line of trees down the middle of the street, and sure enough the guy stopped to get them and we escaped.

Mitch had a knack for scams and getting me involved in them. We were in tenth grade, and we were at a pizza place in Jericho, Long Island.

Mitch convinced the waiter that he'd graduated high school and had already done this and that. The waiter was complaining about wrecking his car.

"My front fender's smashed in and I can't afford to take it to the body shop," he said, so Mitch convinced him that he worked in a body shop. He said he could work on the guy's car from three o'clock to five o'clock on weekdays.

School let us out at 2:45 and Mitch's parents got home at five o'clock, so Mitch picked the guy's car up and had a two-hour window for joyriding.

This went on for a few days. Mitch made it look like he was working on it. He'd spread some kind of putty on it, sand it down or whatever. Mitch didn't know how to fix the car. He just wanted to drive it around for two hours every day.

Mitch picked me up each day and we went joyriding. We kept it in the subdivision because we never saw cops there.

Our friend Larry always stole his parents' car and took us driving, too. So one day we took the waiter's car over to Larry's, and we were revving it and saying, "Come on out! Come on out!"

Larry popped his head out the window over his garage and screamed, "Leave rubber! Leave rubber!"

Then his head jerked back and his mother appeared in the window. "Get that car out of here!"

She had Larry by the neck, but we could still hear him screaming. "Leave rubber! Leave rubber!"

So Mitch wound up the motor in neutral, revving it higher and higher and even higher to impress Larry.

BOOM!

Mitch dropped it into drive, and BOOM!

Something snapped under the car and the two of us as well as the car went flying. It was like a catapult, and we landed on somebody's front yard.

We had been joyriding and abusing the poor car for about a week and the car finally said, "Fuck you!" and catapulted us onto a front yard. The car just flattened out and impaled itself on the lawn. Parts of it were scattered all over.

All of the neighbors and Larry's mom yelled, "Your friends are crazy!" Someone called the police.

We didn't get in trouble because we were so young. I can only imagine the police asking the waiter, "Why did you let the kid take your car?"

———

Mitch was good for mischief, but he was never meant for combat.

We were the same age, but he got left back one grade. I graduated high school and after four months went into the military. I was away for the next two, two-and-a-half years.

During that time, he graduated a year after me and back then, the service waited until you were eighteen-and-a-half years old before they drafted you. So by the time he got drafted, I was already in Vietnam, and we only kept in touch with each other through writing.

He was drafted into the Army, but he wasn't much of a warrior, just not a military type of guy. He got drafted and he was reluctant to go.

His father was not the kind of father who said, "Hey, come on boys! Let's play catch.... What are you doing Saturday? Oh, I'll take you to Yankee Stadium!"

His father wasn't like that. So Mitch never had any guidance on how to deal with the military.

I was away when he got drafted, so I could never give him the dos and the don'ts.

I would have told him to be squared away. He had an opportunity because in the beginning, the Army and the Marines gave intelligence tests. Mitch scored very high. He scored superior. He was too smart to be an enlisted person.

They saw how intelligent he was and wanted to put him through officer's training school. Not only would he have been an officer, but he also would have gone through another year learning to be a helicopter pilot. That's how intelligent he was.

But instead of two years, Mitch would have had to agree to serve for three or four. That was all he could see, and he wanted out as soon as possible. I would have told him to go to school for another year or two, absolutely. It was 1969. The war was going to end sooner or later.

I would've said, "You'll be going to school for maybe a year or two easily, go through officer's candidate school training to be a pilot. That's two years down the road and you'll be in the States, not in Vietnam."

By the time I returned from the war, Mitch had been sent to Vietnam. We only missed each other by a few months. So the last time I ever saw him was June of 1967, right after boot camp. We never saw each other again, just exchanged letters. It was kind of hard to really say your personal feelings in writing.

He didn't last more than four months in Vietnam before he

was killed. Mitch was an assistant machine gunner, which is one of the worst jobs to have. You're just a mule responsible for carrying ammo. On June 3, 1969, his squad was sent on a helicopter to rescue the crew of another helicopter that had been shot down.

Mitch was cut down in a sheet of NVA gunfire as soon as he stepped off, according to D.W. Taylor, who was also on the chopper and received a Silver Star.

Mitch was killed out there in that horrible way. He had barely turned twenty, and he was just too stupid about the military. That killed him. He could have gone to school and been an officer. It would have changed his life positively, and he wouldn't be dead.

His name is etched on the Vietnam Veterans Memorial wall. My daughter traced a copy of it when she went on a field trip to Washington, D.C. in seventh grade. She had no idea what my friend's last name was; she only knew him as Mitch.

She told whoever was in control of looking up names on the wall, "Listen, my father's best friend, I only know his first name. I think he died in 1969."

She found it with just that information. She recognized that last name Sandman, so she brought the tracing home for me.

He always signed his letters with something like, "Yo! Barry! Hang in there, man! Stay cool! Mitch"

I have done my best, Mitch. I have done my best. I hope that I have honored you, and that you would be proud.

35

Home at Last

From 150 Marines in Okinawa, we dwindled to twenty-five in El Toro, California, and five of us were still together on the way to Kennedy airport in New York. One was headed to Brooklyn, one to the Bronx and so on, so we said we'd share a cab ride.

My parents were expecting me, but they didn't know what day or what time. They knew that I was scheduled to be home within two weeks, but I hadn't talked with them in awhile.

The cab took me to within a block of my house in Long Island. It was maybe 2:00 or 3:00 in the morning, a nice, peaceful summer New York night. I shook hands and said goodbye to the other Marines and walked to my house. The lights were off. My parents were asleep.

When you're at war, home is what you live for every hour and every second of every day. To finally stand there in front of my house brought out everything that had built up inside me.

I just stared. It was one of the greatest moments in my life.

The only moment more emotional probably was seeing my daughter born. Other than that, standing there in front of my house in the middle of a New York summer night was the heaviest. I was home from Vietnam in one piece.

I had been more afraid of losing a limb than losing my life. There are times when a mortar is overhead and you jump in a foxhole and you have no control that you just know someone's going to get it. I kept telling myself that I couldn't skate it, couldn't escape it. I knew that I was going to lose a limb.

I just stood there outside the house and took a few minutes to suck it all in.

Of course I was anxious to get in the house and relieve my parents. I knew they were worried sick; every minute that I was away was a burden on them. But at the same time, I wanted to bask in my emotions. They were good, so I stayed there for a few minutes, just soaking it all in.

"Barry, you made it," I told myself. Probably eight or nine months into my tour of Vietnam, I developed a morning ritual. I would take thirty seconds and tell myself, "I have both my hands. I have both my feet. I have both my legs."

So I did the same thing when I got in front of my parents' house. I said, "I am fine. I have all my body parts. This is the moment I've been waiting for, and I made it home in one piece."

36

A Body Bag
for Barry

I only found out after two thugs tried to rob my jewelry store that two vehicles and four people were involved. One never made it out of my store. His other three "buddies" left him lying there with one of my bullets in him and tried to save their own asses.

The mutt in the black trench coat who had jammed the gun in my face only made it out of the store because he wore a bulletproof vest that stopped one of my rounds, even though the shot knocked him to the ground. He drove away in a second car that I never saw. The cops caught the guy that I saw leave in the brown minivan not long after on Route 59. A retired detective heard about the holdup on the police radio in his car and then saw the van. The detective chased him into a Toys 'R' Us parking lot.

The guy jumped out of the van and ran zigzag trying to get away, and he ripped surgical gloves from his hands as he ran. Later on, the cops ask him why he had rubber gloves, and he told them, "Oh, I was supposed to get rid of the jeweler, and I didn't want to get his blood all over me."

They had a body bag for me. Two of them confessed to that. Out of four guys, two confessed that they planned to kill me.

I had a choice of pressing charges of attempted murder or first degree armed robbery, and I chose first degree armed robbery because that holds up better in court.

The guy from the minivan ran into a Wendy's to hide, and when he walked back out, Clarkstown police were waiting and surrounded him, weapons drawn. He spilled his guts, and it didn't take long for cops to track the other two to Danbury, Connecticut, and arrest them.

My main concern at the time was the guy face-down on the floor in the front doorway of my store, half inside and half on the sidewalk. I kept my pistol trained on him and cursed.

"You think you guys are good enough to get over on me?! Who the fuck do you think you are?! You think you can rob me?"

Three police cruisers raced into the shopping center parking lot. A woman cop exited one of them with her weapon drawn, though she didn't aim it directly at me.

"Put your gun down!" she yelled at me.

"I'm the good guy!" I responded. "He's the bad guy!"

My adrenaline was pumping, and I didn't see the cop behind me.

"Put your gun down!" the woman officer ordered me again. That was when I became aware of the cop behind me.

"OK, at least put your gun up in the air," he told me.

I did, and he leaped and grabbed me in a bear hug while another cop approaching from my front lunged and took hold of my pistol hand and pried the pistol away. The officer who had me in the bear hug released me then.

"Do you have a weapon?" he barked at the robber face down on the ground.

"Yes I do," the guy answered. The officer straddled and cuffed him, and then rolled him over and, sure as shit, there was a pistol that the cop immediately took away.

Word came through their radios that the guy from the minivan had been spotted in a Toys 'R' Us parking lot, and with my situation under control, most of the officers headed for there, but it didn't take long for Detective Bill Fritz to show up with a notepad, just like you see on TV. Only five minutes or so had passed since the shootout.

"OK Barry, we're married to each other right now," he told me. "Tell me the story. Give me descriptions. Give me every detail."

He questioned me in his car because my store was now a crime scene. I remember being cold because it was mid-February. A crime scene van pulled in and those officers started blocking off the area with their yellow tape.

I noticed that people passing by in cars were slowing down to see what had happened, and before long, a black car caught my eye.

"I can only advise you," Fritz said to me. "I can't tell you what to do, but I can only advise you not to talk to the press."

"Why would the press come down here?" I thought, and about then, I saw a black car pull in and stop, and my wife jump out. I thought that the police had called her, but really, she had been on her way to a doctor appointment and had just seen my store covered in crime scene tape. She was hysterical.

"Lady, you can't go in there!" an officer said, holding her back.

"Fuck you!" she screamed. "Fuck you! Fuck you!"

She was too upset to get the words "I'm Barry's wife" out of her mouth.

I saw all of that happening from the car in which I was answering Fritz's questions, and I got out and told the one cop that the hysterical woman in front of him was my wife. He bent like a soft banana.

"Ohhh, it's your wife."

By then, paramedics were attending to the thug in my doorway, and by the way they treated him, you'd have thought he was the president of the United States. That bothered me some, a criminal who had meant to kill me being treated that way, but authorities told me later that it was just policy.

It took me awhile to remember the videotape device in my store. It captured everything that went down, and when the cops played it later in the day, they kept saying, "Wow! Oh my God! Oh my God!"

"Let me see!" I said. "Let me see!"

"Barry, you can't."

"Why? It's my tape!"

"You have to go in front of a grand jury, and you have to tell them what happened from memory. The tape would influence you, and it is evidence now."

I accepted that, but something else bothered me, and a little later, I called the detective aside.

"Detective, can I talk to you privately?"

A friend of mine had come in the store the day before with his girlfriend, and she had new breast implants that they both wanted to show off, which she did. So my camera not only had captured the robbery, it also recorded this woman baring her breasts and shaking them at the camera.

"Detective, the whole world is going to know that this girl was shaking her breasts at the camera, and my wife will think I'm involved."

He laughed and told me to relax; they wouldn't show that. I didn't force the girl to stop or anything. I am a male. But after everything that had happened, I could just imagine the shit hitting the fan over the "Big Tits at Barry's Show."

I didn't understand at first when the detective advised me not to talk with the media because I didn't think anyone would care. I soon found out otherwise.

Every TV station in the area called the next day wanting interviews, even offering me transportation. But I heeded the advice and said no. There were too many ways that whatever I said might be turned against me. Still, the video found its way onto national TV, and my store became a popular stop-off for friends and well-wishers.

Someone from Veterans Affairs even called and offered me counseling. He said, "You know, Barry, we can sit down and talk about this over coffee and some cake, and you can tell me every-thing that happened. You can vent.... Would you like to discuss it?"

I was gracious and thanked him for calling, but I really thought, "You think I'm upset about shooting the mutts that tried to rob me?! Fuck them! I don't care about them!"

A cousin even said, "After what you just did, you need to go to counseling. You have to talk to a psychiatrist. You can't just shoot people like that."

But the cops all told me that I did a good job, and some of them even came to tell me their stories about being in similar situations. I guess they felt comfortable about it.

The shootout generated plenty of traffic through my store, but almost no sales. I did hardly any business for that month, but a year later, on the anniversary of the hold-up, it helped give me the idea on how to help a Marine sergeant who was severely wounded fight-ing for our country in Iraq.

He was returned to the States and placed first in a Veterans Affairs hospital, and then a private hospital. The government didn't follow through on promises to help the Marine and his family with their overwhelming needs, and he basically was left to rot. I learned about him and decided to help.

I looked at my record sheet and saw that I'd made almost no money the month of the shooting, February of 2005, and I sur-vived, so I decided that I could do it again. I would take the money that my store made in February of 2006 and donate it to the dis-abled Marine. That's what it boiled down to.

I wear my dress blues during a weekend pass to attend my cousin's wedding. My sister is at left with my mother and my father.

Another Marine and I pose for a Christmas picture in Italy. I enjoyed our "spit and polish" duties as much as I enjoyed the adventure of combat in Vietnam.

I make some sort of grand gesture as we Marines enjoy a few hours of liberty while our ship was in a port in the Mediterranean Sea.

That's me at right as we laugh it up with a drunken Marine who had spent a day of shore leave shopping and drinking during our Mediterranean cruise.

That's me, second from left, serving in the honor guard during my post-Vietnam Mediterranean tour.

I enjoyed honor guard duty on the USS Grant during my Mediterranean cruise.

Standing with my wife Linda
in the mid 1970s, I didn't look
much like a Vietnam veteran
combat Marine.

I managed to save enough of my
Marine Corps pay to buy this
convertible Chevrolet Camaro SS
when I was separated from the armed
services in 1969.

That's me, center, chasing girls and hanging out with
friends at Woodstock. I found it easy to blend in with
civilian life after my tour in Vietnam.

My mentor and squad leader Tom "Ike" Eichler stands behind Captain Earl Breeding, our company commander in Vietnam, at right, and Billy, who lost both legs defending Hill 861-A. We were at a parade honoring Vietnam veterans in Chicago in 1986.

Tom "Ike" Eichler pushes the wheelchair of Billy, who lost both legs in Vietnam, and I'm at the right as we walk in the 1986 Vietnam Veterans Parade in Chicago.

MITCHELL H SANDMAN

My daughter traced Mitch Sandman's name, top of page, from the Vietnam Memorial Wall when she was in seventh grade. Mitch mailed me the photos on this page and opposite while he was in Vietnam in 1969. I received them a few days after he was killed. Mitch gave his life for America; I continue to give mine in order to honor Mitch and all the others who have made the supreme sacrifice for our nation.

CALLS TO DUTY

37

An Honorable Burial

My father, Louis Fixler, inspired me to become a Marine, and after he died on August 31, 2008, we didn't hold an overly religious Jewish service because that just wasn't his personality. He wasn't religious.

He was ninety years old and proud to be an American and proud that he served the country that took him in. When my wife Linda and I arrived in Fort Lauderdale, Florida, for the services, we asked the funeral director if there was any way that we could give him a military burial.

"I'm sorry, Mr. Fixler," the funeral director told me before chapel services, "but that's impossible. We need at least two full days of notice to contact the Army and arrange something like that. We could have if we had known from the beginning, but it is Labor Day weekend, and it's just too late now."

I walked away a little disappointed, but it was the day of the funeral, after all. Linda stayed behind and she and the lady continued to talk.

"You're not Jewish?" she asked Linda, and Linda said, no, she was Italian.

"I'm Sicilian," the lady said. "I'm also Sicilian," Linda answered, and they exchanged high-fives, two women with Italian roots surrounded by a room full of Jewish people. They moved to the edge of the room and continued to talk as friends and family members paid their last respects to my father.

Maybe only an hour passed, and the funeral director came over to me and said, "Barry, bring your car behind the chapel. You'll follow the hearse and lead the procession. It's not far to the cemetery."

I was walking out when I overheard the lady whisper to Linda, "I have a surprise for you."

We arrived at the gravesite to see four uniformed Army soldiers standing at attention. They probably were annoyed at being called to do that on such short notice, and I'll never know how they made it that quickly, but they did. They presented my mother with an American flag, just like you'd see at the funeral for a president.

I couldn't express enough gratitude.

"Thank you very much," I told them. "This is a great honor. My father is a survivor of Pearl Harbor, and I am a Vietnam combat veteran, and right now you are honoring two veterans who fought for this country. I thank you for this honor."

"No, we thank you," the sergeant said, and you had to be me to experience the emotion that passed between us. I saw tears in their eyes, just like in mine.

I was proud of my father, and I always wanted him to be proud of me.

38

The 9/11 Cross

Being a Marine carries responsibilities that last a lifetime, and you never know when or from where a call to duty might come.

I was having a bad day in my jewelry store. I was so busy that I needed my bench jeweler to come up to the counter to help me with customers, and that wasn't going very well. My reputation means everything, and I try to give all customers the time and attention that they deserve.

A bench jeweler is a person who actually makes and repairs jewelry, and mine wasn't happy about being called into customer service. It showed in his attitude. His tone made it clear that he didn't want to be there, that he didn't want to talk, and he could have cared less whether or not he made a sale for me. He was just going through the motions, and I didn't want my customers to sense that. He actually was representing me, and most of my business comes from my hard-earned reputation; most people don't know me personally, but they know my reputation.

People were all over the store looking at jewelry while I showed engagement rings to a couple who had made an appointment, which is time consuming. I was explaining the value of diamonds, the types of mountings, the styles of engagements rings, but all the while I could hear the bench jeweler basically giving my customers the brush-off. He was going through the motions, more people were coming in, and I was getting pissed. I felt the pressure. I was having a bad day.

On top of everything, a conservative looking middle-aged lady with gray hair wandered in, and for the longest time, she just stood there waiting for someone to notice her.

Finally, I excused myself briefly from the engagement couple and walked over to the woman.

"Yes, can I help you?"

She extended her hand and opened it to show me what appeared to me to be two charred nails.

"Sir," she said sweetly, "can you just fix this for me? It's a cross. Could you weld it back together?"

I just looked at her. "Why would you want to do that? It's garbage! It's crap! What would you want to do that for?"

She was quiet at first, and then said, "I'd like to have this repaired and put into a cross."

I snapped back at her: "This is going to cost you twenty-five dollars. It's not worth twenty-five dollars! I have to charge you twenty-fve dollars."

I snapped at her. I was very rude, but she said, "Okay, alright."

So real quick, I grabbed a pen and a work order and I had her fill it out. When she finished, I took the work order and charred nails and put them in an envelope, and then gave her a receipt and she left. That was it.

I went back to what seemed like more urgent matters: taking care of the engagement couple, intervening to smooth things over when I heard the bench jeweler being rude, and basically trying to meet the needs of a store filled with customers.

Finally, around 5:00 p.m., the dust started to settle and I had a little time to think.

"Barry! You just let that sweet, gray-haired lady fall through the cracks and you snapped at her! That's not you!"

I became very concerned and annoyed at myself, and I looked for her repair envelope.

Sure enough, I found it, and I called her immediately to apologize.

I'm sorry that I don't remember her name, but let's say it was Mary.

A woman answered the telephone and I said, "Hi. My name is Barry. May I speak to Mary please?"

"This is Sister Mary."

That threw me off. She was a nun. She was dressed conservatively when she came in the store, but nothing about her had indicated that she was a nun.

"Hi, Sister Mary, this is Barry the jeweler. I'm calling to apologize to you that I was rude to you when you were in my store."

"Yes, I know," she said, "and I'm sitting here writing a letter stating that I have never met a mean Marine before you."

She said that she had heard that I am a very patriotic Marine, and she just wanted to come in specifically to do business with me.

I didn't know that, of course. I apologized again. "I'm so sorry that I snapped at you. The repair job will be ready in a week."

Her tone turned pleasant and she accepted my apology.

When she came back a week later to pick up her cross, I had it welded together and polished. It looked great. Now it looked like a cross.

Sister Mary looked very pleased. "Well, how much?" she asked.

"No, after what I did to you, I'm not going to charge you," I answered.

Then she told me the story behind the cross, and why she had come to me, a jeweler who also was a Marine who fought for our country.

"This cross is sacred," she said. "It came from 9/11. I found it on the ground next to a church and it was burnt. The heat made it fall apart, but the two pieces stayed together, so I picked them up and brought them to you to make whole again."

I was overwhelmed. This was something very important, sacred, and I had almost blown it.

39

Saving Faith
in America

A Marine from near where I live was shot in April of '05 in Iraq. It was a miracle that he made it home, but when he did, the U.S. government didn't take care of him. I learned about him through my wife, Linda, who is a nurse at Helen Hayes Hospital in West Haverstraw, New York, where the Marine was transferred. I went to see him, as one Marine to another, to give my thanks, and through his parents found out that the Department of Veterans Affairs was sweeping him under the rug.

That was when I made him my cause, and more people than I could have imagined made him theirs, too. Americans do care. They proved that to me, and they proved it to the young man and his parents.

We focused on one wounded Marine then—his name, his face, his family—but those things aren't so important now because he is well known and has an active base of supporters. However the story of this wounded Marine is important because there are thousands of wounded warriors and families of heroes out there who are in need of help but suffer silently in a state of virtual anonymity.

The Marine was shot in the head by friendly fire during an early morning mission. A .30-caliber bullet lodged in his head. He actually died on the battlefield and was revived by his fellow Marines, his parents said.

He was a corporal at the time, and six other Marines from his sniper team were on the roof of a building where the Marines were holding an Iraqi family that they had been tasked with placing under protective custody. Reports indicated that 150 or more insurgents were in the immediate vicinity and a tank crew that was supposed to be supporting the sniper team somehow mistook the Marines on the roof for bad guys.

Combat is chaotic and mistakes—friendly fire incidents and collateral damage   are inevitable

Tragically, the U.S. tank shot the Marine in the head twice, his parents said. One bullet entered and exited his jaw. The other bullet entered his head and made a mess of his frontal lobes as it traveled through his brain, eventually lodging in the other side of his skull. Another Marine heroically used his own body to shield his comrade while the radio operator called to stop the friendly fire.

The young man died on the roof that morning, but the heroic Marines wouldn't give up on him. They performed CPR on him and revived him, his parents said, and four of them carried him down off the roof to a waiting Humvee that drove them through the hostile city. From the edge of the city, an Army Blackhawk helicopter evacuated him to Al Quaim for emergency medical treatment, then on to Balad.

Doctors there looked at the Marine and saw little hope. But a physician who was a general saw the wounded man move his arms and legs in a way that indicated he was not brain dead, his parents said, and the surgeon had him moved from the triage group written off for dead to an operating table where he removed the bullet from the Marine's head. The general did not give up.

They stabilized the Marine enough to fly him to Germany but he still wasn't expected to survive. His parents were flown to Germany so that maybe they could be with him before he died.

Even as the parents were en route to Germany, parishioners at their church in upstate New York began organizing a prayer for him that quickly spread through the Internet to thousands of people. The prayer request was also picked up by talk shows. "Please pray for (this Marine) tonight," was a plea heard and acted upon by millions of Americans as the parents flew across the Atlantic to see their son possibly for the last time.

When they arrived in Germany and rushed to his side, they didn't even recognize him; his head was swollen and his face was covered in gauze and bandages.

The tattoos on his chest and arms were the only way that they could be sure that it was him. But the young man was tough, and his condition stabilized enough to fly him back to the States and a Navy hospital in Maryland.

The doctors in Iraq and Germany were wonderful. They did a great job just in keeping him alive, and they were good when he first got back over here and he was in a Naval hospital in Bethesda, Maryland. But the Marine's progress stopped after he was transferred to a VA hospital in Virginia. It just stopped. His body was contracting into a fetal position, and he was getting bed sores.

His parents were understandably frustrated. It was as if their son was stowed away on a shelf in a VA warehouse to rot and die. His parents said that he was so neglected at the VA hospital that it was not uncommon for them to find him covered with flies.

"How can we stand here and watch our son deteriorate and die?" his mother asked herself.

The wounded Marine was wasting fast, and so his parents started contacting politicians trying to get their son out of the VA hospital and into a private hospital where he could get more attention. Finally, U.S. Representative Sue Kelly was able to get him moved to Helen Hayes Hospital in West Haverstraw.

That's when my wife told me about him.

"You got to be kidding me," I said to her. "A Marine at Helen Hayes?"

"I think he got shot in Iraq," she said. At the time he was the only active-duty Marine that we knew of who ended up in Helen Hayes.

I had to immediately go visit him. His mother was there hovering over him, and her son was curled in a fetal position just staring into space, unable to talk.

I introduced myself to the mother, and I tried to tell the Marine how proud I was of him, but he couldn't communicate back, and that made me uncomfortable. I came back two days later and I brought a red Khe Sanh hat that was very dear to me. I gave it to him.

Now, he couldn't talk, but he could look at me, and he did.

"This hat is very dear to me," I told him. "I went through the Siege of Khe Sanh, and here's this hat."

I kissed his mother—we really didn't know each other yet—and told the Marine again how proud I was of him. After about fifteen minutes, I left.

When I went back a week later, his mother had put up a shelf to hold all of the gifts that people had given her son. She re-introduced me to him.

"Son, do you know who Barry is?" she asked him. His eyes zeroed in on my Khe Sanh hat.

"Oh my God, Barry!" she said. "My son knows you! He knows you because he's staring at your hat!"

That was a sure sign of progress to her, that her son knew what was happening around him.

I kept going back just to show my support and let the young man know that people out there cared about him. Here was a Marine who was wounded protecting our country, and I wanted him to know: Americans do care.

I was getting to know his mother a little, but I had no idea that the family had financial problems. She told me about how the doctors in Germany had wanted to pull the plug on her son, but she refused to give up on him. And again at the Navy hospital in Maryland, the neurosurgeon had advised them to take him off life support. "Even if he lives, he will never recognize you," the doctor said. "He won't know you're his parents."

"I will not let my son die," the mother insisted. "He may not remember that I am his mother, but I will never forget that he is my son." So the neurosurgeon did his best, and when the Marine came out of a four-month-long coma after the surgery, his mother was there by his side. Doctors said he wouldn't remember his parents, but he looked at her and whispered, "Mom."

One day his mother and I were in the Marine's hospital room and she started talking about how she wished that the federal government was as interested in her son's well-being. She felt as if they were being brushed under the carpet.

"I feel like I'm a leper," she said. "You call the government and you get no one to talk to. You know, I need help. How about when my son gets better? My son needs physical therapy; my son needs mental therapy. My son is going to have special needs, and my home is not equipped for that.

"My house is old. It's not equipped. The government promised us fifty thousand dollars, but we haven't seen it. Right now, I can't bring my son home."

That caught me off guard, that the government was dropping the ball and that she thought that its promises are meaningless. She was as frustrated as could be.

235

At that time, I thought that the government would take care of him as best as possible for his lifetime. I was never wounded, so like many Americans, I didn't know much about VA hospitals. Whatever exposure that I had to the VA was decades old, from Vietnam, and I just figured that the VA takes care of everything. Not true.

Now we're at war again, and seeing men and women sent home wounded is new to a lot of people. Times have changed. Problems have changed.

Hearing the fallen Marine's mother talk about it all made me decide that I would try to do something, whatever I could.

We were a couple of months away from the first anniversary of my shootout in the jewelry store, and the local community had been so wonderful to me in the time since: awards, dinners, honors, phone calls. The recognition had been overwhelming, beyond my imagination, so I already had been thinking about what I might do in return to show my gratitude.

Boom, a light went on: The wounded Marine! The Marine was in trouble and his parents were in trouble. I would give back through him.

I would not give back by saying thank you for my store; I would give back by saying thank you through the wounded Marine. I focused on him. His parents were feeling like lepers, as if America didn't know that they existed. I said, "Well, you are going to exist now."

"The government dropped the ball," I thought, "but I am an American, and America is not going to drop the ball. We're going to come up with the fifty thousand dollars that his parents need so that they can get their house ready and bring their son home."

The first week or ten days were frustrating, like beating my head against a wall, but I was relentless. When I'm plugged in, I am focused, focused, focused.

Unfortunately, not many people in Rockland County knew who the wounded Marine was. Just his name alone meant nothing to anyone.

So I had his mother give me pictures—her son in his dress blues, that sort of thing—and put them on everything that I had printed, gave a face to the name: "This is our Marine. He got shot in Iraq protecting our country, and now he needs our help and his family needs our help."

I took out newspaper ads. I had thousands of fliers printed. I even bought billboard space.

Then I went on a speaking tour, from the Rotary to the Boy Scouts, to the Marine Corps League to the Veterans of Foreign Wars and to the American Legion, and so forth. I even spoke to the motorcycle club where I'm a member. It was all about the injured Marine.

A week later, the big idea hit me. I would have a Valentine's Day sale in my store, and all of the proceeds from the sale and the fundraiser would go to the young man and his family.

I placed a huge Plexiglas box in the store where people could make their donations. It was decorated with an American flag and pictures of the Marine; that was his spot.

The young man's name started getting out on the streets.

I had a tent erected in the parking lot outside the store because it was too small and so many people were coming in. I had coffee and hotdogs in the tent; it was February, so I had a portable outdoor heater, too. Twelve Marines came in their dress blues to show support. They were from my old unit in Garden City, New York; from South Jersey; from Newburgh, New York.

I needed the Marines, their wounded comrade needed the Marines, and Marines came, just to stand there all day in their dress blues and thank everyone and be proud. Semper Fi.

I only planned to have the tent there for two or three days, but that turned into seven, and then ten. I finally had to take it down because it took up the whole parking lot, and that made my neighbor store owners nervous. They knew it was a fund-raiser and they knew where I was coming from, but I couldn't take business away from everyone.

Guys would come in and say, "I don't have a girlfriend or a wife to buy jewelry for, but can I make a donation?"

The money came from all directions and in all denominations: $2, $5, $10, $20, $50, $100. It was very contagious.

One guy called to ask how much I charged for an appraisal. He had no idea what was going on. I told him $100, and when he came in and saw all of the commotion, he asked what it was for and I told him. He not only gave me the $100 for the appraisal, he doubled it and said, "That goes to the Marine." He couldn't believe that the government wasn't taking care of our wounded veterans.

The parents knew that I was raising money for their son, but I didn't promise them a certain amount of money, like the $50,000. In fact, I hadn't even told them about the Valentine's Day sale, but his father still heard about it on his construction site in White Plains, New York. I had only met the father once, briefly, and he came over to the store while everything was going on. It caught him totally off guard. When I told people who he was, they all turned around to shake the man's hand and his knees almost buckled. He couldn't shake hands. He had to hug everyone.

One morning a construction worker showed up at the door of my store. He was huge, and he was covering his eyes, and I saw him and thought, "No way am I letting this guy in."

I came to the door, and he kept his eyes covered and just held out three $100 bills. He tried to compose himself and said, "I just found out what you're doing for that wounded Marine. I don't know him personally. In fact, I never heard of him, but I just can't believe the government is not doing what it's supposed to do."

He just handed me the $300 and bolted. He was overwhelmed and his emotions took over, and he didn't want me to see him crying.

The guy had no reason to be ashamed. The young man's story touched many people, and they came from everywhere to offer their help to a Marine whom they didn't even know. It was a totally new experience for me.

Another time, early in the morning, I didn't even have the store lights on yet and heard knocking at the door.

"I know you're in there, Barry! The guy over at the deli said you got coffee already! I know you're in there!"

I saw a construction truck in the parking lot, and the guy at the door was holding out $500.

"I just heard what you're doing for that Marine who was shot. I don't know him, but I know that you're doing this for a wounded Marine, and here's five hundred dollars."

"Well, thank you, thank you," I said, "but don't move! Give me your name, something. I have to send you a thank you."

"No, no, I don't want a thank you."

"Well, give me something."

"I don't want a thank you," he said, "but I'm going to give you my card. I'm in construction; I do cement work. I only want a call that I can come and help with anything that Marine needs. I'll help with construction. That's the only reason that I'm going to give you my card, in case the Marine and his family need my kind of help."

I'm telling you, it was contagious. When I spoke to the VFW, the crowd mostly was World War II guys who were in their eighties. I had talked to my wife, Linda, at home before the speech and told her that I was sure that the VFW would give something for the Marine, probably $100 or $200, and that would be really nice.

"You know what?" she answered. "They are America's greatest generation; they'll give you four hundred dollars."

"No way! They aren't going to give me four hundred dollars. They're old and on fixed incomes."

Those World War II guys at the VFW didn't have a clue about the wounded Marine; they'd never heard of him, but his story touched their hearts.

"Alright," the post commander said. "We're going to make a donation!"

They started talking among themselves after I finished my speech, and the group leader said, "We'll take five hundred dollars out of our checking account."

I protested the large amount of money, but another member trumped me.

"We should take out a thousand!"

"No, no, no! I didn't come here for that kind of money!" I said.

"I think we should raise it to fifteen hundred dollars," another man said.

"No, no, no!" I argued. "C'mon, you guys are on fixed incomes. You don't have that kind of money. Maybe a few hundred dollars, not fifteen hundred."

"Hey, don't listen to him!" someone else said. "Let's go to two thousand."

Then the post commander took charge.

"I'm going to give Barry a check for twenty-five hundred dollars for this wounded Marine," he declared, and then while I protested again, he asked for a show of hands in favor or against. Every hand shot up in favor of $2,500. The VFW gave $2,500.

I couldn't wait until the next day to show the Marine and his mother the check.

I felt as if I had hit the lottery. I could have sold $20,000 in jewelry over the counter of my store and not felt as good as I did holding that $2,500 check for a Marine in need. That's the high that I got.

I probably spent $10,000 of my own money to get the word out. Some people asked me why I spent my money on advertising when I could have just given it to the Marine and his parents. I told them that my $10,000 just would have been a Band-Aid, that the family needed a lot more.

And I wanted people to know about the Marine and his family, and to know that many others like him are out there. And I wanted the family to know that America cares. Giving them $10,000 couldn't have done that. I was focused on raising $50,000, for the Marine and his family, from the public, and I wasn't going to give up until I did.

We raised almost $19,000 in the first week, and things snowballed from there. The local TV stations caught on and came to do stories. Newspapers jumped in. The Marine's name started to become recognizable around my area.

We counted the donations at the end of every week, and I wouldn't even touch the money with my own hands. I'd have it put in a big bag and drive it over to the hospital for the young man's parents to count.

We raffled a motorcycle that netted $22,500. A friend of mine, Colonel Jack Hussey, solicited pledges and swam across the Hudson River. He raised a little over $20,000 just by doing that.

Between those two events, benefits, the store donations and the contributions from the different organizations where I spoke, we topped $100,000, and word spread so far that the Marine was featured on HBO. His became a household name. People know he exists, that his family exists, and they have shown that they care more than the government ever did.

The Marine can talk now, and he is still making progress as his brain heals and reorganizes itself. Doctors are amazed at his progress. Groups and individuals from all over the country make sure that he and his family receive the care and attention that they need. If we had left everything up to the government, he would still be in a hospital staring at the ceiling.

I have been especially gratified to see what all of this has done for his parents, to see the change in his mother as her son has gradually progressed from that sad state he was in.

But I can't leave things at that. We only helped one Marine, one family, and far too many veterans like him are out there suffering with their overwhelmed families. There are wounded warriors who sacrificed their lives to protect America from terrorists and are wasting away in VA hospitals. America needed them and now they need America. They need people to step up and give them a face, a voice and support.

That's why I have pledged to raise $1 million from the proceeds of this book to help wounded combat veterans and their families. I take my pledge very seriously. I'm focused.

But I'm just one American, and $1 million is just a start. I need you. They need you.

In my heart, I feel that I can definitely and positively raise $1 million from this book to give to wounded combat veterans. I figure, if I could raise $100,000 just for one Marine and his family, I can, with the help of America, make a difference for our many other wounded veterans and bring attention to the brave young warriors who sacrificed everything and have received not nearly enough in return.

I hope you all agree. That would be truly Semper Cool.

I stand with my hands of the shoulder of Joseph Golden, the 2008 Rockland County, New York, Veteran of the Year, during my own award ceremony for the same honor in 2009.

My wife Linda and I pose with Police Commissioner Ray Kelly, center, at the 2007 Marine Corps Ball at The Pierre hotel in New York City.

Joe "Cisco" Reyes, in the football jersey, poses with his family, our former squad leader Tom "Ike" Eichler, front right, and me during the 2010 Khe Sanh Veterans Reunion in San Antonio. Reyes received three Purple Hearts, while Ike received two and one Silver Star.

I'm the guy in the tie shaking the hands of active duty and veteran Marines who came to my jewelry store to support my fund-raiser for a wounded Marine.

This proclamation made me proud.

Hanging out with my grandson Ryan at a New York Yankees game, above. My daughter Desiree's high school graduation picture, below.

My mother was overwhelmed with emotion when I dedicated my Veteran of the Year award to my father, who passed away one year earlier.

My father looking sharp in his Army dress uniform
at Pearl Harbor, Hawaii.

My father, center, with his Army buddies on an island in the Pacific
during World War II.

I was always so proud of my father.

APPENDIX

AUTHOR'S NOTE AND
ACKNOWLEDGEMENTS

I have done my best to write this memoir honestly and accurately. I relied on my memories and on the recollections of my fellow Marines. We did not keep journals or log books and many stories of heroism and courage were left on the battlefield. Combat is a close companion of chaos, and therefore minor discrepancies are inevitable, but I held myself to a standard of under-exaggeration and I am confident that I have captured my experience of the Vietnam War as accurately as humanly possible. It is my sincerest hope that my fellow Vietnam veterans are as proud of this book as I am of their service, sacrifice and camaraderie.

The Marines I fought with are some of the best and bravest men our country has ever offered. Many of their lives were cut short by enemy fire, but they did not die in vain and they are not forgotten. I owe my life to the Marines who mentored me and to those who led us in combat. I am humbled by the bravery and selflessness of the Marines I fought with in Echo Company. You are all heroes to me.

I thank my mother Ronnie, my wife Linda, my daughter Desiree and her friends Tania and Tara, my grandson Ryan and my godson Ross for their support. I thank the many advance readers who offered valuable feedback and constructive criticism. I thank the Lucas family for permission to use Mike's photos and their contribution to the success of *Semper Cool*.

Writing a book is a monumental task, but it is only the beginning. *Semper Cool* would not have been possible without my publisher, Taylor Dye, and his team of editors, including Dan Murray, James Wade and Sharon Nettles. My original manuscript was more than 600 pages of war stories that Taylor's team was able to weave into a flowing narrative while preserving the tone and voice of my writing. I give them credit for the strengths of this work and take personal responsibility for any of its shortcomings. I thank my personal publicist and friend Lisa Feuer for her many contributions, suggestions and support.

Finally I want to thank the people of the United States of America and the current generation of warriors who have volunteered to protect our freedoms. Every dollar I earn from this book belongs to those of you who were physically wounded fighting for America in Iraq and Afghanistan. Financial requests should be made through my foundation at: www.sempercool.com/bff. I am proud of all of you, and your country is grateful.

Stay cool!
Barry

NATIONAL POW/MIA
RECOGNITION DAY

The third Friday of September is National POW/MIA Recognition Day. Many Americans would like to honor our nations Prisoners of War and Missing in Action, but are not sure how. I suggest setting a traditional remembrance table at your family dinner, or requesting one be set at your favorite restaurant. The tradition takes only a few minutes and is a small but meaningful gesture to those who have perhaps made the ultimate sacrifice for our country.

Here is a list of the items required:

- Small American Flag
- Small round table
- White tablecloth
- Single place setting
- Pinch of salt sprinkled on plate
- Wine glass – inverted
- Slice of lemon on bread plate with a pile of spilled salt
- Small bud vase with a single stem red rose
- Red ribbon tied around the vase
- White candle – lit
- Empty chair

This is a suggested passage to be read, or considered:
This table is our way of symbolizing the fact that brave Americans are missing from our midst. They are commonly called POWs or MIAs, we call them "warriors." They are unable to be with us this evening and so we remember them.

This Table, set for one, is small and symbolizes the frailty of one prisoner alone against his oppressors.

The Tablecloth is white and symbolizes the purity of their intentions to respond to their country's call to arms.

The single rose in the vase signifies the blood they may have shed in sacrifice to ensure the freedom of our beloved United States of America. This rose also reminds us of the family and friends of our missing warriors who keep the faith, while awaiting their return.

The vase is tied with a yellow ribbon and represents the yellow ribbons worn on the lapels of the thousands who demand with unyielding determination a proper accounting of our comrades who are not among us tonight.

The lit candle is symbolizes the light of hope which lives in our hearts to illuminate their way home, away from their captors, to the open arms of a grateful nation.

A slice of lemon is on the bread plate to remind us of their bitter fate.

The salt sprinkled on the plate reminds us of the countless fallen tears of families as they wait.

The wine glass is inverted because they cannot toast with us this night.

The chair is empty. They are not here.

The American Flag reminds us that many of them may never return - and have paid the supreme sacrifice to ensure our freedom.

Let us remember - and never forget their sacrifice.

May God forever watch over them and protect them and their families.

ABOUT THE AUTHOR

Barry Fixler is a U.S. Marine Corps veteran who served in Vietnam in 1967 and 1968 and fought on Hill 861-A during the legendary Siege of Khe Sanh. After receiving an honorable discharge from the Marine Corps in 1973, Fixler used the G.I. Bill to finance his undergraduate degree from the Gemological Institute of America and joined his father in the jewelry business. Today he lives with his wife Linda in Bardonia, N.Y., where he owns Barry's Estate Jewelry.

Barry has long been aware of his good fortune and has made point of sharing it. He has aided numerous wounded Marines and soldiers, to whom his loyalties are obvious, but has also helped people who have had no connections to the military. In recognition of his good citizenship and humanitarian efforts, Barry was named 2009 Veteran of the Year by the Rockland County Veterans Coordinating Council.

Barry is donating all of his royalties from *Semper Cool* to physically wounded combat veterans and the families of our fallen warriors. You can learn more about Barry's foundation, The Barry Fixler Foundation, and monitor the progress of his million dollar goal on his Web site: www.sempercool.com. You can also watch the video of the Valentine's Day attempted armed robbery and gunfight.